Yum!

TASTY RECIPES FROM CULINARY GREATS

COMPILED BY JEFFREY SPEAR & DARA BUNJON

EDITED BY JULIA M. PITKIN

PRESENTED BY

YUM! TASTY RECIPES FROM CULINARY GREATS
Published by Cumberland House Publishing, Inc.
431 Harding Industrial Drive
Nashville, TN 37211

Cover design by JulesRulesDesign
Text design by Julie Pitkin
Photography by Vince Lupo / Direction One, Inc.

Library of Congress Cataloging-in-Publication Data

Yum! : tasty recipes from culinary greats / compiled by Jeffrey Spear and Dara Bunjon ; edited by Julia M. Pitkin ; photography by Vince Lupo ; presented by Microplane.
     p. cm.
   Includes index.
   ISBN 978-1-58182-616-6
   1. Cookery. I. Spear, Jeffrey. II. Bunjon, Dara. III. Pitkin, Julia M. IV. Microplane (Firm) V. Title.

TX714.Y698 2007
641.5—dc22

2007020991

Printed in China
1 2 3 4 5 6 7 — 13 12 11 10 09 08 07

Dedication

This book is dedicated to our brother Tim, who loved fine food, Christmas, and superheroes. His battle with kidney disease too often kept him confined to a bed instead of out saving the world. So instead, he spent his time refining his drawing skills. His memory is a great source of courage and determination in all our lives.

Chris Grace (CEO)
Microplane®

Artwork by Tim Grace

Contents

Acknowledgments

This cookbook represents a tremendous amount of generosity throughout the culinary community. When contributors learned that Microplane® would donate 100% of its profits from the sale of this book to the National Kidney Foundation (www.kidney.org)*, they were more than happy to participate.

Microplane® wishes to thank all of these culinary experts—from chefs and restaurateurs to writers, educators and marketers—for their support with this endeavor. Our heartfelt thanks and appreciation goes out to (in alphabetical order): Jody Adams, José Andrés, Nancy Baggett, Dan Barber, Najmieh Batmanglij, Rick Bayless, Renee Behnke, Riccardo Bosio, Miriam Brickman, Dara Bunjon, Jennifer Bushman, Shirley Corriher, Eric Crowley, Ariane Daguin, Francois Dionot, Tom Douglas, Nathalie Dupree, Elizabeth Falkner, Susan Feniger, John Fleer, Susanna Foo, Kat Fukushima, Joyce Goldstein, Gael Greene, Dorie Greenspan, Joanne Gregory, Penny Grey, Jamie Gwen, Susan Hermann-Loomis, Cindy Hutson, Barbara Kafka, Sheilah Kaufman, Christine Keff, Helene Kennan, Faye Levy, Nick Malgieri, Ti Adelaide Martin, Judy Mattera, Leslie Meyer, Mary Sue Milliken, Sara Moulton, David Myers, Haley Nguyen, Nona Nielsen-Parker, Joel Olson, Roland Passot, Scott Peacock, Caprial & John Pence, Nora Pouillon, Joanna Pruess, Steven Raichlen, Michel Richard, Suvir Saran, Whitey Schmidt, John Shields, Hiroko Shimbo, Anna Sortun, Reggie Southerland, Jeffrey Spear, Susan Spicer, Jose Torres, Rick Tramonto, Jerry Traunfeld, Karen Trilevsky, Charlie Trotter, Ming Tsai, Norman Van Aken, Annie Wayte, Joanne Weir, Dede Wilson, Roy Yamaguchi and Sherry Yard.

Aside from our sincerest thanks to each and every one of the culinary experts whose recipes grace the pages of this book, there are a few other organizations and individuals we would like to thank.

We tested and evaluated more than 100 recipes to make this book happen. Needless to say, our home kitchens could hardly support or endure the rigors of this effort. Fortunately, and through the generosity of LaDeana Litchfield—Maryland Hospitality Education Foundation (www.mhef.org), Diana Hegmann and Bette Mullins—Eastern Technical High School and the Maryland ProStart program (www.mhef.org), we were given access to the professional kitchen and culinary facilities at Eastern Technical High School. Let's just say that hospitality and generosity of this nature exceeded anything we could have imagined.

Additionally, and as part of their culinary training, the junior class of culinary students at Eastern Technical High School participated in recipe testing and helped us complete our efforts accurately and in a timely manner. We'd like to thank them all (in alphabetical order): Casey Ardoin, Crystal Clark, Jessica Danenmann, Britani Devin, Katie Donahoe, Derica Dowd, Tabitha Hubbel, Joseph Laflame, Dominique Law, Morgan Markley,

Timothy McFarland, Lisa Ndubuisi, Crystal Palmer, Chrystina Prestianni, Andrew Schmitz, Brittany Turner, Andrea Ulrich, Zachary Ulrich, Kathryn Weinkam, Malcolm Williams, Ronald Williams and Julia Zingarelli.

Lastly, we received professional culinary support from Nona Nielsen-Parker, Leslie Meyer, Joanne Gregory and Janice Shih, all established culinary professionals who graciously volunteered to help us get the job done. Without their experience and insights, we'd still be in the kitchen.

On behalf of everyone involved, our profound and warmest thanks. We couldn't have done this without you.

* To learn more about the National Kidney Foundation, kidney disease and organ donation as well as make contributions, please visit: www.kidney.org.

About Microplane®

As Founder of Microplane®, Richard Grace is right at home checking out displays in a kitchen store or shaking hands at culinary trade show. As a young man, it wasn't exactly where he pictured himself, but he's very grateful to be there.

By now, cooking aficionados worldwide are familiar with the story: A Canadian housewife commandeers one of her husband's favorite wood working tools and discovers it effortlessly produces the lightest, most wonderful orange zest she could have ever imagined. It's 1994, her Armenian Orange cake is a huge success and her husband's Microplane® rasp has morphed into a 'must have' kitchen grater. It seemed as if a star was born overnight, but it didn't happen quite that fast, in fact, it took over thirty years.

It was the 1940's. Michigan native Louis Grace, a tool and die maker in Detroit, started a shop with his two brothers. As was the case for many families, the war came along and everything changed. The business closed and the brothers were forced to go their separate ways to provide for their families. Over the years Louis dreamed of restarting the business with his son Richard, but Richard felt the priesthood calling and headed to Boston to attend the seminary. After several years of study, Richard realized that he was more interested in airplanes and creating things than studying. He returned home to Michigan, pursued an engineering degree, and went into business with his father.

In 1967, Louis and Richard started Grace Engineering Inc. in Memphis, Michigan. The young company struggled. Knowing the Grace's plight, their local priest graciously offered to loan them $10,000 from an inheritance. "To us it was divine intervention," said Richard. "Without the help from Father Charlie, I'm not sure we would have made it." The company soon turned things around and was hired to make a part for a computer printer company. "The part was very difficult to make, so we gave him a price of $6 dollars each. He thought the price was ridiculous and felt we were trying to get rich on the job" remembers Richard. However, after months of searching, the engineer was unable to find anyone willing or able to manufacture the part. He came back to the Graces and asked if the $6 price was still good. Grace Engineering was off and running.

By 1976, the booming printer industry was going through growing pains. Richard felt that many of the parts could be made more efficiently using a chemical etching process which would require different equipment and a specialized building.

Having grown tired of the long hard Michigan winters, Richard and his own young family set off for the fairer climate of Arkansas. When asked how they learned the chemical etching process, Richard replied, "We bought the equipment and a book about it. It was a good thing we had no idea how difficult it was because we probably never would have done it!"

Soon laser printers came on the market and the parts Grace manufactured quickly became obsolete, Richard remained optimistic. He had seen a lot of companies try to use the chemical etching concept to make cutting tools, but no one was able to develop a reliable manufacturing process. After several years of trial and error, they succeeded. Grace Manufacturing, as the company was now known, named their new line of woodworking tools Microplane®. The tool line was a success and Grace Manufacturing became world renown for their quality craftsman tools—until that day when their best-selling rasp accidentally turned into a kitchen grater.

With just a few modifications, and a slight change in their marketing plan, an entire new product line of graters for home cooks and professional chefs was introduced. The response was extraordinary. Since that time, Microplane® graters have distinguished themselves from other graters by using that patented chemical process to create ultra-sharp cutting edges. Unlike stamped graters, they effortlessly cut through hard and soft foods without tearing or shredding.

Now celebrating their 40th anniversary, the company continues to develop innovative woodworking and kitchen tools, and, at the urging of loyal customers, the company has developed a revolutionary new foot file for the personal care industry.

Father Charlie's extraordinary gesture to Louis Grace has never been forgotten. Although Richard Grace never became a priest, the company he helped build still does business by adhering a familiar biblical passage from the book of Luke that states, "For unto whom much is given, much shall be required."

Grace Manufacturing and the entire Grace family generously support many charities and non-profit organizations including the National Kidney foundation. Your support of this cookbook is greatly appreciated. *Bon appetit!*

If you'd like to learn more about Microplane®, its renown culinary zesters, graters and slicers, or to find out where to purchase any of these products, please visit www.microplane.com or call Customer Service at 1-800-555-2767.

Grating and Zesting

For years, Microplane®'s Classic Series Zester has been recognized by professionals throughout the restaurant and foodservice community around the world as one of the top ten, must-have, culinary tools. In addition, the name Microplane® has become synonymous with the act of zesting and is frequently used in recipes as a verb (ie. to "Microplane®" a lemon) when fine citrus zest is the desired result.

What has not been fully realized, is that Microplane® has a wide range of culinary tools that have been designed, not only for zesting, but for grating and slicing all sorts of cooking and baking ingredients.

All of the recipes in this book utilize a zester, grater or slicer of one description or another in their preparation. Understanding that every chef has his or her own preferences, and out of respect to individual tastes, we have not specified which Microplane® tool is best for any particular task. Accordingly, we've prepared some brief product descriptions to help you select the right tool with the right blade for the right job.

 Medium Ribbon - Designed to work in both directions to save valuable time, this tool is perfect for grating soft cheese as well as butter when preparing pastry. It's also the right choice for grating hard foods such as chocolate for baking and decorating and cabbage for no-hassle slaws.

 Coarse - Instantly transforms Parmesan and other hard cheeses into perfect shreds. It is also ideal for grating coconut, ginger and onion.

Extra Coarse - An extremely efficient tool, perfectly designed for grating cheddar and other soft cheeses, as well as all sorts of fruits and vegetables, such as apples, green papaya, daikon and potatoes.

 Fine - Ideal for zesting lemons and limes without lifting off the fruit's bitter tasting pith. This is also the essential tool for finely grating nutmeg, cinnamon and nuts or preparing a fine mince of ginger.

 Zester - This is the tool that made Microplane® famous. Perfect for zesting all types of citrus. It produces light and fluffy wisps from both Parmesan cheese or chocolate, creates ultra-fine morsels of garlic and ginger instantly, and shreds coconut for baking and decorating.

 Zester/Grater - This is Microplane®'s number 1 best-selling kitchen tool. In fact, it's considered one of the top ten "must-haves" for the professional chef or home cooking enthusiast. It is perfect for zesting citrus, creating airy wisps of Parmesan and finely grating ginger. It effortlessly yields delicate bits of cinnamon, chocolate or nutmeg for baking and garnishing.

 Small Shaver - Creates light and fluffy shavings from Parmesan and other hard cheeses as well as delicate wisps from chocolate that are perfect for baking and decorating. It also delivers exceptional results when grating apples, butter, garlic and onion.

 Large Shaver - This culinary workhorse delivers fast shavings of chocolate for baking recipes and garnishes. It also grates a wide range of hard and soft foods quickly and easily.

Special Ingredients

We know that, while our contributors are all culinary experts, their recipes may not have been written down — they merely exist in their imagination and are artfully produced without blinking an eye. In other situations, proportions were scaled for restaurant use where hundreds of portions are made at a time.

To make sure these recipes are appropriate and perform in your kitchen, we've tested each and every one. Unless a unique ingredient was specified in any of these recipes, the butter we used was always unsalted, eggs were Grade A large and flour was All-Purpose. All temperatures are degrees Fahrenheit.

You may also encounter ingredients that are exotic, unusual, ethnic in origin and conceivably hard to obtain in your neighborhood. We've provided a few definitions (below) that will help you better understand the nature of these items and where you can find them. It has been our experience that, when local supermarkets, grocery and specialty stores did not stock what we were looking for, the internet was a fabulous resource for additional information and purchasing opportunities.

Here are just a few of the ingredients we thought you'd like to know a little more about (in alphabetical order):

'00' White Flour - This is a designation used by Italian flour producers to describe how finely the flour has been milled. Tipo 00 is typically used to make bread, cookies and other baked goods. We found Tipo 00 flour at the local Italian specialty store as well as online.

Barberries - Barberries add a delightfully tart, tangy and lemony flavor to a wide range of dishes. They are an especially important ingredient in Iranian dishes, including a wedding specialty where the sourness of barberries reminds us that life is not always so sweet. In the Ukraine, they are used as flavoring in a popular candy of the same name. In Iran, the dried fruit is also known by its Persian name: Zereshk.

Benimosu - This is a purple sweet potato vinegar sweetened with honey. It is similar to sherry vinegar and quite popular in Japanese cooking. It can be found most easily via the internet.

Bitto - This is a variety of cheese that comes from the high alpine region of Italy known as Valtellina. It's distinctive flavor comes from, in part, the fact that cows free graze and consume the wild herbs that grow in alpine pastures. Bitto cheese can be found in Italian specialty stores, gourmet cheese shops and through the internet.

Black Soybean Miso - Also known as kuro-daizu miso, this is a unique product made from black soybeans. It has a distinct, milder bean flavor that makes this ingredient quite different from the more commonly available red and yellow varieties. Depending on the Asian influence in your neighborhood, you may find this product easier to obtain through the internet.

Capers - Capers are the unopened green flower buds of the Mediterranean caper bush, a bushy plant with culinary origins from the region including France, Italy and Algeria. They range in size from that approximating a peppercorn to significantly larger. They are generally packed in a vinegar and salt brine with a taste that is both pungent and astringent. While they are widely available in mainstream supermarkets, specialty and ethnic stores may offer greater variety in terms of size and geographic origin.

Caperberries - While capers are the unopened green flower buds of the caper bush, caperberries are the fruit that follows after the caper flowers. While their flavor is not as strong as the caper, they also come packed in a vinegar and salt brine. Just about any supermarket or specialty store will stock this popular ingredient.

Chihuahua Cheese - This is one of many varieties of Mexican cheese. Quesillo and Asadero are good substitutes, as are Monterey Jack and Fontina. You can find these cheeses in supermarkets that cater to their Latino neighbors as well as specialty (ethnic) grocery stores.

Chipotle in Adobo Sauce - Adobo is a moderately spicy, dark red sauce. Chipotle in Adobo Sauce is typically packed in cans and found in either ethnic grocery stores or the international aisle in mainstream supermarkets.

Court Bouillon - This is a liquid used primarily for poaching - especially fish. A basic recipe consists of water, white wine, lemon, salt, bouquet garni and black pepper. With so many variations available, we recommend you search the internet to see what recipes are available.

Crème Fraîche - (French for "fresh cream") Similar to sour cream, this originally French food is a heavy cream slightly soured with bacterial culture. Unless there is a high demand, this item is not typically stocked in mainstream supermarkets. It is, however, available in most specialty grocery stores.

Creole Mustard - This is a regional recipe, one in a seemingly endless array of mustards available today. It is a whole grain variety with a little spicy zest typical in Creole cooking. While readily available in Louisiana and its neighboring states, it can be difficult to find in other regions. We had the best luck finding this product online.

Fish Sauce - Also known as nam pla, fish sauce is a pungent condiment made from fish that have fermented in brine. While not palatable on its own, it is an essential ingredient in many Southeast Asian cuisines. Fish Sauce is easy to find in Asian grocery stores and is frequently stocked in the "international aisle" in mainstream supermarkets.

Geoduck Clam (pronounced "gooeyduck") - Also known as "Mirugai" or "Giant Clam." Not all seafood markets carry this item, even in ethnic neighborhoods. We found local sushi bars and the internet to be our best resource.

Green Papaya - While papaya is readily available in most supermarkets, this is the green, unripened fruit. In some Asian grocery stores, the green fruit is sold in a separate bin, apart from its ripe brethren. It may also be available pre-shredded for use in salads and other recipes.

Green Tea Matcha (also spelled Maccha) - This is a powdered green tea used to color and flavor many Japanese foods including soba noodles and green tea ice cream. While not as ubiquitous or inexpensive as the many leaf variety of green teas currently flooding the stores, it can be found in Asian supermarkets in with all of the other tea products.

Hoisin Sauce - This is a dark, sweet Chinese dipping sauce that accompanies Mu Shu Pork, Peking Duck, Barbecued Pork and Spring Rolls. It is widely available in supermarkets as well as Asian grocery stores.

Lemongrass - This somewhat woody, thin stalk has a distinctly citrus flavor (hence its name) and is widely used in Asian cooking. Quite popular in the United States, it can be found in most mainstream supermarkets and Asian grocery stores in the fresh produce section. If it is not readily available as fresh, the frozen stalks perform equally well.

Mache - This is arelatively unknown salad green, also known as field salad or lamb's lettuce. From an agricultural perspective, it is heartier and can be harvested in late fall and early spring when other varieties of fresh greens are harder to find. Ask the greengrocer at your favorite specialty food store to see when these greens are available.

Maldon Sea Salt - There is a noticeable difference in flavor between regular table salt and sea salt. This is the soft, white and flaky variety of sea salt made by the Maldon Sea Salt Company in England. It is completely natural, made without artificial additives, and has a distinctive flavor and texture unlike other types of sea salt.

Ogo Seaweed - This is an edible variety of seaweed most commonly used in Asian salads or as a garnish. It comes in a variety of colors and can be found in Asian grocery stores, most likely in the Japanese food section. In Hawaii, it is known as "limu loa."

Pink Peppercorns - Pink peppercorns are the dried fruit of the Baies Rose and are not a true peppercorn. They have a peppery flavor and are becoming increasingly popular amongst professional chefs and home cooking enthusiasts. While not readily available in mainstream supermarkets, they can be found in most specialty (boutique) grocery stores.

Pomegranate Molasses - Don't confuse this with the thinner, overly sweet Pomegranate syrup (Grenadine) that is often used in cocktails. This is a thicker, brown substance with a more concentrated and somewhat tart flavor. It is also referred to as Dibs Roman or Dubs Rumman and is available in Middle Eastern specialty stores.

Scotch Bonnets - These fiery peppers are related to the Habanero. Unlike the orange Habanero, Scotch Bonnets are scarlet red when fully mature. Originally from the Caribbean, they add heat and a unique flavor to a variety of recipes including Jamaican dishes including jerk pork or chicken.

Truffles - These are highly prized, aromatic delicacies with a price tag to match. They have a rich aroma and flavor unmatched by any other substance. Depending on quality and geographic origin, they can easily retail for more than US $300 per pound. Fortunately, this popular fungus is used in very small quantities and will not break the bank. Although harvested in many places around the world, a majority comes from France and Italy.

Turkish Red Pepper Paste - This spicy condiment is made from red capsicum and chilies and can be found in Middle Eastern and European specialty stores. There are also numerous recipes available through the internet to make your own.

ADDITIONAL RESOURCES

While there is a seemingly endless supply of online resources to help you obtain that special recipe or hard-to-find product, these are a few of the sites we rely upon and find most helpful on a regular basis:

www.penzeys.com
www.epicurious.com
www.melissas.com
www.igourmet.com
www.dibruno.com
www.amazon.com
www.orientalpantry.com

Conversion Tables

We know that Microplane® kitchen graters are enjoyed around the world. Anticipating that this cookbook will be enjoyed in countries utilizing metric, instead of imperial standards, we have provided this table to help convert ingredient quantities. While measures are accurate regardless of where you are, there may be subtleties in ingredient quality that will influence outcomes. This is especially true when working with flour and eggs.

OVEN TEMPERATURES

°F	°C
250°	120°
300°	150°
325°	160°
350°	180°
375°	190°
400°	200°
450°	230°

CUP AND SPOON MEASURES

Note: There is a difference between fluid ounces and ounces of weight. That is why there are dry and liquid measuring tools. It is also important to remember that the weight of an ingredient varies, depending on the ingredient measured (i.e.: 1 cup of chopped parsley is much lighter in weight than 1 cup of sugar).

The correct way to measure dry ingredients is to spoon them into a dry-measure cup.

1 Cup	250 ml	8 fluid ounces	
½ Cup	125 ml	4 fluid ounces	
⅓ Cup	80 ml	2½ fluid ounces	5⅓ Tablespoons
¼ Cup	60 ml	2 fluid ounces	4 Tablespoons
1 Tablespoon		20 ml	
1 teaspoon		7 ml	
¼ teaspoon		1.25 ml	

LIQUID MEASURES

Imperial	Metric
1 fluid ounce	30 ml
2 fluid ounces	60 ml
3½ fluid ounces	100 ml
4 fluid ounces	125 ml
5½ fluid ounces	170 ml
6½ fluid ounces	200 ml
7 fluid ounces	220 ml
8 fluid ounces	250 ml
9½ fluid ounces	300 ml
10 fluid ounces	315 ml
11 fluid ounces	350 ml
12 fluid ounces	375 ml
13 fluid ounces	410 ml
14 fluid ounces	440 ml
15 fluid ounces	470 ml
16 fluid ounces	500 ml
20 fluid ounces	600 ml
25 fluid ounces	750 ml
32 fluid ounces	1 L (1000 ml)

DRY MEASURES

Imperial	Metric
½ ounce	14 g
1 ounce	28 g
1½ ounces	43 g
2 ounces	57 g
2½ ounces	71 g
3 ounces	85 g
3½ ounces	99 g
4 ounces	113 g
5 ounces	142 g
6 ounces	170 g
7 ounces	198 g
8 ounces	227 g
12 ounces	340 g
16 ounces (1 pound)	454 g
1 pound 8 ounces	680 g
2 pounds	900 g

Appetizers

CARPACCIO WITH ARUGULA, SHAVED PARMESAN, & MUSTARD-CAPER SAUCE

BY NORA POUILLON • SERVES 4

1	TABLESPOON MUSTARD
1	TABLESPOON SMALL CAPERS
1	TEASPOON BALSAMIC VINEGAR
1	TABLESPOON OLIVE OIL
	FRESHLY GROUND BLACK PEPPER
½	POUND EYE OF THE ROUND, PARTIALLY FROZEN TO FACILITATE SLICING
2	OUNCES PARMESAN CHEESE, SHAVED
4	OUNCES ARUGULA, WASHED, SPUN DRY, AND CUT IN JULIENNE

Make the mustard-caper sauce by putting the mustard, capers, and vinegar into a small bowl. Add the oil while whisking with a fork to emulsify the sauce. Season to taste with pepper.

Cut the eye of the round into the thinnest slices possible with the sharpest slicing knife you own. (You could also ask a butcher to slice the meat into thin slices for you)

To assemble, spread a thin layer of the mustard sauce on the center of 4 chilled salad plates. Cover with overlapping layers of sliced beef.

Arrange the Parmesan shavings over the center of the layered beef slices. Garnish with a mound of arugula.

Serve cold.

ABOUT NORA POUILLON

www.noras.com

Nora Pouillon, a true believer in a sustainable lifestyle, is a long-time advocate for increasing the quality and nutritional value of the food supply. She is the chef and owner of two of Washington, DC's most popular restaurants. Featuring organic multi-ethnic cuisine, the internationally known Restaurant Nora opened in 1979 and has been praised for its delicious, high quality healthy food. Nora's second restaurant, Asia Nora, serves uniquely interpreted dishes from across Asia using organic ingredients. In April 1999, Nora became the first certified organic restaurant in the country, which means that at least 95% of all the ingredients served in the restaurant are certified.

Nora Pouillon has been a crusader for clean food since the early 70's when she first became aware of conventional farming practices and the use of chemical additives, pesticides and hormones in food. Her goal—to show people that healthy clean food is delicious tasting—developed into a campaign for organics and a more sustainable lifestyle. Nora is also an advocate for cleaner oceans, the preservation of our fish population, and other environmental issues.

ACHIEVEMENTS

- *Cooking with Nora* cookbook (Park Lane Press)
- Chef of the Year – Award of Excellence by the International Association of Culinary Professionals (IACP)

Q: What is your favorite comfort food?
A: Dark sourdough rye bread with good country butter.

Q: What put you on the culinary career path?
A: My Austrian parents who taught me the importance of fresh, seasonal, healthy cooking.

Q: If you were condemned to die, what would be your last meal?
A: Good American Sturgeon caviar and Champagne from a small house.

MANGALORE FRIED SHRIMP

MANGALORE FRIED SHRIMP

BY SUVIR SARAN • SERVES 4

This dish is from the southern Indian coastal state of Karnataka, where seafood is an important part of the diet. The shrimp has extraordinary flavor. I sometimes vary the recipe by adding 1½ tablespoons unsweetened, shredded coconut along with the mustard seeds, or 2 to 6 chopped, small fresh green chilies with the scallions.

1	POUND MEDIUM SHRIMP, PEELED AND DEVEINED
½	TEASPOON CAYENNE PEPPER
¼	TEASPOON GROUND TURMERIC
¼	TEASPOON MUSTARD POWDER
2	TEASPOONS FRESH LEMON JUICE
4	TEASPOONS CANOLA OIL
½	TEASPOON BLACK MUSTARD SEEDS (OR CUMIN SEEDS)
6	FRESH (10 FROZEN) CURRY LEAVES, TORN INTO PIECES (OPTIONAL)
1	1-INCH PIECE FRESH GINGER ROOT, FINELY GRATED
3	TABLESPOONS FINELY CHOPPED SCALLION
	SALT, TO TASTE

Rinse the shrimp and pat them dry on paper towels. Put them in a bowl and sprinkle with the cayenne, turmeric, mustard powder, and lemon juice. Stir gently to coat the shrimp evenly with the spices. Cover and refrigerate for 30 minutes.

When the shrimp have marinated, combine the oil, mustard seeds (or cumin seeds), and curry leaves (if using) in a large wok, frying pan, or kadai over medium-high heat. Cover if using mustard seeds (the seeds splatter and pop) and cook until the cumin darkens and/or you hear the mustard seeds crackle, 1 to 2 minutes. Add ginger and cook for 1 minute more.

Add the shrimp and cook for 30 seconds, stirring often.

Add the chopped scallion and cook, stirring, until the shrimp turn pink all over, about 1 minute. Sprinkle with salt and serve hot.

ABOUT SUVIR SARAN

www.americanmasala.com
www.indianhomecooking.com
www.devinyc.com

Suvir Saran, New Delhi-born chef, teacher and cookbook author, has already become a respected food authority at age 34, and is poised to make a lasting impact in the food industry. Saran established new standards for Indian food in the United States when he teamed up with co-chef Hemant Mathur in 2004 to create the authentic flavors of Indian home cooking at Dévi in Manhattan, which received a one-star rating in the Michelin Guide New York City 2007, three stars from New York Magazine and two stars from *The New York Times*.

In 2006, he began a partnership with Sodexho, a leading global foodservice company, as its first-ever "International Concept and Brand Development Partner" to work side-by-side with Sodexho's chefs and operators for culinary training and business development; and bring international foods, flavors and innovative culinary techniques to the workplace.

Author of the widely acclaimed *Indian Home Cooking: A Fresh Introduction to Indian Food, with More Than 150 Recipes* (Clarkson Potter/Publishers), Saran teaches for such culinary centers as Sur La Table, Cooks of Crocus Hill, Apron's at Publix and Institute for Culinary Education; and has been invited to speak at prestigious institutions such as the Culinary Institute of America, NYU Department of Nutrition and Food Studies, and the Smithsonian Institution. He is also a contributing authority to Food Arts Magazine. His upcoming cookbook, *American Masala,* will be published by Clarkson Potter in October 2007.

He resides in New York City and in upstate New York, where he has a farm.

Q: If not for food, where would you be now?

A: I got into food by accident. I had always wanted to be a singer, doctor or artist. Once I landed in the U.S., I realized Indian restaurants served food I was familiar with but it never appealed to me. That led me to host dinners at home. Friends that came found a new love for food and a new look into the world of Indian cuisine. Of course, that led me to where I am today. It would still be a treat for me to go to medical school and become a doctor. I also love teaching. To become faculty at a well respected college or university would be thrilling and fulfilling.

SCALLOPS WITH SALSA CRUDA AND GREMOLATA

BY GAEL GREENE • FROM HER BOOK *INSATIABLE: TALES FROM A LIFE OF DELICIOUS EXCESS*
SERVES 4

SAUCE

4 GREAT LARGE BEEFSTEAK
TOMATOES
¼ CUP MINCED SHALLOTS
1 TABLESPOON OLIVE OIL (TO
COOK SHALLOTS)
2 TEASPOON MINCED CILANTRO
OR PARSLEY
1 TABLESPOON EXTRA VIRGIN
OLIVE OIL (FOR TOMATO MIX)
1 TEASPOON LEMON JUICE
¼ TEASPOON COARSE SALT (OR TO
TASTE)
FRESHLY GROUND PEPPER

GREMOLATA GARNISH

2 CLOVES GARLIC, MINCED
1 TEASPOON OLIVE OIL (OPTIONAL)
¼ CUP MINCED PARSLEY
1 LEMON, FINELY ZESTED

SCALLOPS

12 LARGE SEA SCALLOPS
⅓ CUP VERY FINE FRESH
BREADCRUMBS
¼ TEASPOON SALT
FRESHLY GROUND PEPPER
3 TABLESPOONS BUTTER

To prepare the sauce: Blanch, peel and seed tomatoes and squeeze out the juice (reserve for another use). Chop, drain any liquid, and reserve.

Sauté the shallots in olive oil until soft but do not let color. Remove from the heat. Stir in the chopped tomatoes and cilantro or parsley. Season the sauce to taste with extra virgin olive oil, lemon juice, salt, and pepper.

To prepare the gremolata: The garlic may be sautéed lightly in a little olive oil if raw garlic frightens you. Mix together the garlic, parsley, and lemon peel.

To prepare the scallops: Pat the excess moisture off the scallops. Shake the scallops in a brown paper bag with the breadcrumbs, salt, and pepper to coat. Sauté in hot butter very quickly on both sides until the edges are golden and they are warm and still rare inside.

To serve: Arrange three scallops per plate with sauce and gremolata.

Note: Don't make this dish unless you have great summer tomatoes. It also works with really fresh swordfish cut into 1-inch cubes. It is also wonderful on linguine and then might serve 4 as a lunch entrée.

For more years than she likes to admit, Gael Greene was the Insatiable Critic for *New York* magazine where she helped change the way New Yorkers think about food. Certainly she had an effect (for better or worse) on the language of food writing. A scholarly anthropologist could trace the evolution of New York restaurants on a time line that would reflect her passions and taste over 30 years—from the snooty Le Pavillon of Henri Soulé to the truffle fields of France to nouvelle cuisine to couturier pizzas, pastas and melting chocolate cake, to more healthful eating. She continues to write about restaurants for *New York* in her weekly column, "Insatiable Critic." She is also the author of seven books, including two best selling novels, *Blue Skies, No Candy* and *Dr. Love.* Much sensuous eating, dancing and living spice up her memoir, *Insatiable: Tales from a Life of Delicious Excess* (Warner Books, 2006), which documents four decades of how America fell in love with food. Twenty-five years ago, Ms. Greene and the late James Beard co-founded Citymeals on Wheels which, by December 2006, has delivered thirty four million meals to New York's homebound elderly who now number 17,500.

- 2006 *Insatiable: Tales from a Life of Delicious Excess,* Warner Books
- 2000 International Association of Cooking Professionals magazine writing award
- 1992 The James Beard Foundation Humanitarian of the Year
- 1986 *Delicious Sex,* Prentice Hall Press

PHOTOGRAPH BY DAN WYNN

Q: What put you on the culinary career path?
A: I am sure I was born hungry. I could never get enough love, attention or puréed banana. I was a foodie before that word even existed, rushing off to France for cuisinary epiphanies. My then husband and I were a folie a deux of foodies.

Q: If you could eat anywhere in the world, where would it be?
A: New York City is the best place in the world to eat right now but my mouth needs to visit France at least once a year.

Q: What is your favorite family recipe?
A: I am famous among my pot luck party pals for my fruit crumble—plum or blueberry in summer, Granny Smith apple or apple and dried fruit in winter.

SCALLOPS WITH SALSA CRUDA AND GREMOLATA

BEETS, CAVIAR, APPLE, HORSERADISH

BY ELIZABETH FALKNER • SERVES 4

2	MEDIUM BEETS
2	TABLESPOONS OLIVE OIL
	SALT
1	TEASPOON ZINFANDEL WINE
	VINEGAR
1	TEASPOON HONEY
	FRESHLY GROUND PEPPER
½	GRANNY SMITH APPLE, CHILLED
2	TABLESPOONS CRÈME FRAICHE
1	TO 2 OUNCES CALIFORNIA
	OESETRA CAVIAR
½	CUP MICRO CELERY OR OTHER
	MICRO GREENS
1	KNOB FRESH HORSERADISH ROOT
1	LEMON OR MEYER LEMON

Wash and scrub the beets and set in a casserole. Sprinkle on olive oil and salt. Cover and roast at 350° for 45 minutes to 1 hour, or until easily pierced. Remove from the oven and allow to chill completely.

Reserve the beet juices in the casserole.

Remove the skins from the beets (they should easily slip off) and trim the ends. Slice the beets in thin round slices and divide on 4 plates. I like to line them up as in a deck of cards, slipped.

Combine the beet juices with the vinegar and honey and a little pepper. Drizzle over beets.

Grate the Granny Smith apple over the beets in a stack in the center of the beets.

Smear a small spoonful of crème fraiche in front of the beets.

Place a spoonful of caviar at one end of the crème fraiche.

Scatter a few micro greens over each plate.

Grate horseradish all over the plate, like snow.

Grate a little lemon zest on the beets.

Cut a lemon in half and squeeze a little on each plate.

Wine note: Serve with Champagne.

ABOUT ELIZABETH FALKNER

www.citizencake.com

www.citizencupcake.com

Hard work, determination and a unique vision have made Elizabeth one of the most celebrated pastry chefs in the United States and influential food professionals in the Bay Area. Citizen Cake is located in San Francisco's eclectic and vibrant Hayes Valley.

Elizabeth began her professional cooking career in 1990 as the Chef of Café Claude, moving quickly into the pastry department at Masa's, under Chef Julian Serrano in 1991. By 1993, Elizabeth became the pastry chef at Elka/Miyako Hotel before moving on to Rubicon.

Recognizing the need for a contemporary, quality pastry shop in the Bay Area, Elizabeth opened the first Citizen Cake in San Francisco in October 1997. Citizen Cake is a retail patisserie featuring contemporary cakes, chocolates, pastries and ice creams all made in house. Citizen Cake is also Elizabeth's imaginative restaurant and bar, serving brunch, lunch and dinner. In 2004, Elizabeth opened Citizen Cupcake, a satellite café featuring many signature Citizen Cake items.

Television appearances include: "Iron Chef America," "Bravo's Top Chef," "Tyler's Ultimate," "Rachel Ray's $40 a Day," "Food Network Challenge," "Sugar Rush," "Best Of," "Bay Café," and more.

In 2007, Elizabeth and her life partner, Sabrina Riddle will open a new restaurant, "Orson," on 4th and Bryant streets in San Francisco. Orson will be a 150 seat restaurant and bar featuring live DJ's, cocktails, multiple courses and shared plates in a sexy "living room" space designed by Zack/deVito architects.

ACHIEVEMENTS

- 2006 "Pastry Chef of the Year," *Bon Appetit*
- 2005 Nominated "Best Pastry Chef" for a James Beard Award
- 2003 "10 best pastry chefs in America," *Bon Appetit*

Q: What is your favorite comfort food?
A: Chocolate chip cookies.

Q: If not for food, where would you be now?
A: Another artistic driven business such as architecture or film.

Q: If you could eat anywhere in the world, where would it be?
A: Japan.

SPICY GARLIC & LEMON CRUSTED SHRIMP

BY TI ADELAIDE MARTIN • SERVES 4

1	POUND LARGE WILD AMERICAN SHRIMP, PEELED WITH TAILS LEFT ON
8	CLOVES GARLIC, GRATED
2	EACH SHALLOTS, GRATED
2	TABLESPOONS GROUND BLACK PEPPER
1	TABLESPOON KOSHER SALT
1	LEMON, FINELY ZESTED, CUT IN HALF AND JUICED
8	SPRIGS FRESH THYME
2	TABLESPOONS WORCESTERSHIRE SAUCE
2	TABLESPOONS HOT SAUCE
½	BOTTLE DARK BEER (I.E. ABITA AMBER OR BASS)
2	TABLESPOONS PLUS 2 TABLE-SPOONS UNSALTED BUTTER

Combine the shrimp, garlic, shallots, black pepper, salt, lemon zest, lemon juice, thyme, Worcestershire sauce, hot sauce and beer in a large bowl and mix. Cover with plastic wrap and refrigerate for 1 to 6 hours.

To cook, place a large skillet on the stove over high heat for 2 minutes or until very hot. Add 2 tablespoons of butter to the pan and add the shrimp and the marinade all at once, stirring constantly. Cook for 4 minutes or until the shrimp are pink and the small bits of garlic and shallots are golden brown.

Remove the shrimp from the pan, reserve on a warm serving platter, and swirl the remaining 2 tablespoons of the butter into the sauce. The sauce should be thick, brown, and shiny with bits of caramelized garlic, thyme, and black pepper. Spoon the sauce over the shrimp and serve with warm crusty French bread or over pasta or rice. This make for a wonderful hors d'oeuvre.

Serving Suggestions: Serve with crusty bread, pasta, or rice.

Q: If you were condemned to die, what would be your last meal?
A: There is no question—my last meal would be an oyster poboy dressed. Lots of hot sauce, perfectly / lightly fried oysters, great French bread, and fresh creole tomatoes.

Q: What put you on the culinary career path?
A: What put me, and a lot of other people, on my culinary career path was watching my mother's passion for this business. Her intense focus on pushing an entire group of people to be the very best at something, and the great fun she and we all have in the process.

ABOUT TI ADELAIDE MARTIN

www.commanderspalace.com

Food has always played a major role in Ti Martin's life. Ti grew up going to work in her family's restaurants alongside her mother, Ella Brennan. Her first job, at the age of ten, was stamping "souvenir" on the restaurant's menus. Stints in the kitchen, at the front door and even in the dish room followed.

Family gatherings were always centered around food—making crab salad after crabbing, taking cooking classes together, and going on restaurant chasing trips. Thus, it's only natural that Ti has built her career around food.

After graduating from Newman School and Southern Methodist University in Dallas, Ti received her Masters in Business Administration from Tulane University in 1984.

In 1991, Ti teamed up with her cousins, Brad and Dickie Brennan, to open Palace Café, chosen by *Esquire* magazine as one of the top new restaurants in America that year. In 1997, Ti returned to Commander's Palace to join Lally, Brad, Ella and Dottie Brennan at the family's flagship restaurant.

Ti is an integral part of the signature Commander's experience. She seems to radiate an innate sense of true Southern hospitality, creating lasting memories for diners day after day.

Ti's latest venture, Café Adelaide and the Swizzle Stick Bar, is again, a family collaboration. Much like its namesake, Adelaide Brennan or "Auntie Mame" as they called her, the restaurant is "worldly-wise with New Orleans roots," dishing up a playful take on Creole cuisine.

ACHIEVEMENTS

- 2005 Honorary Doctorate, Business, Loyola University New Orleans
- 2000 *Commander's Kitchen* cookbook receives James Beard nomination
- 2000 City Business' Women of the Year Award, *City Business*
- 1999 50 New Tastemakers, *Nation's Restaurant News*

> Q: If you could eat anywhere in the world, where would it be?
>
> A: If I could eat anywhere in the world it would be New York's River Cafe. It's known for the view—unbeatable—but Buzzy provides the quintessential big deal dining experience in terms of exquisite food, professional service, and great hospitality. They get forgotten—but to me I have had several of the most memorable meals of my life there—including recently. He does it all, and the view ain't half bad.

QUESO FUNDIDO CON CHORIZO Y RAJAS

MELTED CHEESE CASSEROLE WITH MEXICAN SAUSAGE AND ROASTED CHILES

BY RICK BAYLESS • FROM HIS BOOK: *MEXICO ONE PLATE AT A TIME*
SERVES 6*

2 FRESH POBLANO CHILES

4 OUNCES MEXICAN CHORIZO SAUSAGE (½ CUP), CASINGS REMOVED (STORE BOUGHT OR HOMEMADE)

1 MEDIUM WHITE ONION, SLICED
SALT

12 CORN TORTILLAS, THE FRESHER THE BETTER (STORE BOUGHT ARE OK, THOUGH HOMEMADE WILL SHINE)

8 OUNCES CHIHUAHUA OR OTHER MEXICAN MELTING CHEESE SUCH AS QUESADILLA OR ASADERO (LACKING MEXICAN CHEESE, QUESO FUNDIDO IS DELICIOUS MADE WITH EVERY-THING FROM MONTEREY JACK TO MILD CHEDDAR), SHREDDED OR GRATED (YOU'LL HAVE ABOUT 2 CUPS)

1 TEASPOON CRUMBLED DRIED OREGANO, PREFERABLY MEXICAN

Roasting the poblano chiles: Roast the poblanos on an open flame or on a baking sheet 4 inches below a very hot broiler, turning regularly until the skin is evenly blistered and blackened, about 5 minutes for an open flame, about 10 minutes for the broiler. Be careful not to char the flesh-only the skin. Cover with a kitchen towel and let stand for 5 minutes. Rub off the blackened skin, then pull or cut out the stems and the seed pods. Tear the chiles open and quickly rinse to remove stray seeds and most bits of skin. Cut into ¼-inch-wide strips about 2 inches long.

To prepare the chorizo-poblano mixture: Heat the oven to 350°. In a medium-size skillet (preferably non-stick), cook the chorizo over medium heat, stirring to break up any clumps, until half-cooked, about 5 minutes. (As the chorizo heats, it should render enough fat to cook the meat; if the mixture seems dry, add a little oil.) Add the onion and cook, stirring frequently, until the onion is richly golden and the chorizo done, about 10 minutes. (If the mixture looks very oily, drain.) Stir in the poblano strips. Taste and season with salt as needed. Transfer the mixture to a 9- or 10-inch shallow baking dish, Mexican cazuela or pie plate.

Finishing the queso fundido: Very lightly dampen a clean kitchen towel. Check the tortillas to make sure none are stuck together. Wrap them in the towel, then in foil, sealing the edges tightly. Place in the oven and set the timer for 7 minutes.

When the timer goes off, stir the cheese into the warm chorizo mixture. Set in the oven alongside the tortillas and bake until the cheese is just melted but has not begun to separate or look greasy, about 5 more minutes. Sprinkle with the crumbled oregano and serve immediately, accompanied by the warm tortillas.

Working Ahead: The chorizo-poblano mixture can be made a day ahead, covered and refrigerated; warm it in your baking vessel before stirring in the cheese and baking. Queso fundido doesn't hold well, so don't put it in the oven until everyone is ready to make tacos.

*__Note:__ This recipe makes enough queso fundido for 12 soft tacos, serving 6 as an appetizer, 4 as a casual main dish.

QUESO FUNDIDO CON CHORIZO Y RAJAS

ABOUT RICK BAYLESS

www.fronterakitchens.com

Award-winning chef-restaurateur, cookbook author, and television personality Rick Bayless has done more than any other culinary star to introduce Americans to authentic Mexican cuisine and to change the image of Mexican food in America.

Rick is fourth generation in an Oklahoma family of restaurateurs and grocers. From 1980 to 1986, after studying Spanish and Latin American Studies, and doing doctoral work in Anthropological Linguistics, Rick lived in Mexico with his wife, Deann, writing his now-classic *Authentic Mexican: Regional Cooking From The Heart of Mexico* (William Morrow, 1987). *The New York Times* hailed this work as the "greatest contribution to the Mexican table imaginable."

In 1987, Rick opened the hugely successful Frontera Grill, specializing in contemporary regional Mexican cooking.

On the heels of Frontera Grill's success, Rick opened Topolobampo in 1989. Adjacent to Frontera Grill, Tobolobampo is one of America's only fine-dining Mexican restaurants. Frontera Grill and Topolobampo have received glowing distinctions from *Gourmet, Food & Wine, Bon Appétit, Atlantic Monthly, Condé Nast Traveler* and many others. Topolobampo has been nominated twice by the James Beard Foundation as one of the most outstanding restaurants in our country.

In 1996, Rick began the prepared food line of salsas, chips, and grilling rubs under the Frontera Foods label. Frontera Foods went on to open Frontera Fresco, a food kiosk in the Marshall Fields building in 2005 in Chicago.

Rick resides in Chicago with his wife and daughter. With his wife he runs Frontera Grill and Topolobampo. He is on the board of Chef's Collaborative and has been active in Share Our Strength.

ACHIEVEMENTS

- 2006 *Mexican Everyday* cookbook receives James Beard nomination
- 2004 *Rick & Lanie's Excellent Kitchen Adventures* (Stewart, Tabori & Chang)
- 2001 *Mexico One Plate at a Time* (Scribner) wins James Beard "Best International Cookbook"
- 1996 *Rick Bayless's Mexican Kitchen* (Scribner) wins IACP National Julia Child "Cookbook of the Year Award"

Q: What is your favorite comfort food?
A: Anything in a tortilla!

Q: If not for food, where would you be now?
A: If I weren't a chef, I would be a writer.

Q: If you could eat anywhere in the world, where would it be?
A: In my back yard with my family and friends.

FRONTERA GRILL

CHEESE DELIGHT

BY SHEILAH KAUFMAN • SERVES 8

½   POUND GRUYERE CHEESE, GRATED

½   POUND SWISS CHEESE, GRATED

1   TABLESPOON DRY WHITE SHERRY

¼   CUP PLAIN YOGURT

1   BUNCH GREEN ONIONS, MINCED

2   CLOVES GARLIC, MINCED

1   LEMON, FINELY ZESTED

¼   CUP MINCED RED ONION

¼   CUP MINCED PARSLEY

In a large bowl combine the cheeses, sherry, yogurt, green onion, garlic, and lemon zest. Mix well, cover and refrigerate for an hour, overnight, or up to two days.

When ready to use, preheat broiler, and spread on bread slices, or stuff in mushrooms. Combine red onion and parsley in a small bowl and sprinkle on top. Broil until golden brown and bubbly.

Serving suggestions: Put the cheese mixture on bread, stuff it in mushrooms, tomatoes, or omelets. This is a great do-ahead delight.

Q: What is your favorite comfort food?

A: My favorite comfort food is dark chocolate, usually baked in a rich bread pudding, or in my sinful decadent brownies.

Q: What put you on the culinary career path?

A: I was born with a sweet tooth and a severe craving for chocolate, (unfortunately), into the wrong family. My mother's idea of sweets was a vanilla wafer or a piece of un-iced sponge cake; my idea, on the other hand, was eat the icing and throw away the cake. I wanted anything that was made of dark/semisweet chocolate. My problem was solved when, at the age of eight, my mom taught me how to bake. I started with brownies and rapidly progressed to chocolate cakes, fudge and a variety of chocolate cookies.

CHEESE DELIGHT

ABOUT SHEILAH KAUFMAN

www.cookingwithsheilah.com

Bringing the flavors of the world into homes and kitchens is
Sheilah Kaufman's greatest gift. As the author of 25 delectable
cookbooks and a traveling culinary instructor for more than 38
years, Sheilah has shared her great passion for richly flavored,
easy and elegant food and cooking with thousands of home chefs
across the nation (from Alaska and Hawaii, to Mexico). Known by
students and home chefs as the spokeswoman for all things "fearless and fussless," Sheilah brings to the table uniquely refreshing
and creative recipes that are practical and easy while maintaining a
delicious elegance. As one newspaper editor said "Sheilah is a
treat! From soup to nuts, she's a pro. Her cooking classes are fun
and fast-paced with recipes and hints you'll use for years. As for
her cookbooks, the wide-range (of topics) fills every need. Sheilah
Kaufman is fabulous."

A prolific writer and editor, Sheilah has written for numerous
magazines and papers, including *Vegetarian Times* (articles on
Cooking with Beer, Chanukah, and Turkish Cuisine), and *The
Washington Post*. She was the fancy food and gourmet editor for
Gift and Dec Magazine for more than 20 years. She is the food editor
for *Jewish Women International* and is a contributing food editor for
the *Town Courier*. Sheilah has developed recipes for Beatrice Foods,
Smucker's, and Walden Farms.

A founding charter member of the International Association of
Culinary Professionals, Sheilah also is an active member of Les
Dames d'Escoffier.

PHOTOGRAPH BY JACKIE SAUTER

ACHIEVEMENTS

- 2007 *Upper Crusts: Fabulous Ways to Use Leftover Bread* cookbook
- 2003 *Simply Irresistible: Easy, Elegant, Fearless, Fussless Cooking* cookbook
- 2003 *A Taste Of Turkish Cuisine* cookbook
- 2002 *Sephardic/Israeli Cuisine* cookbook

SHRIMP COCKTAIL

BY RICK TRAMONTO · SERVES 4

4   MEDIUM UNSEASONED COOKED
    SHRIMP, PEELED AND DEVEINED
1   TABLESPOON CELERY SALT
4   OUNCES BLOODY MARY MIX,*
    CHILLED
2   OUNCES VODKA, CHILLED
1   PIECE FRESH HORSERADISH
    (ABOUT 1 OUNCE)
1   TABLESPOON CHOPPED SCALLION
    TOPS

Slice each shrimp into bite size pieces.

Rim 4 "shot" glasses with celery salt.

Place one sliced shrimp per shot glass. Cover each shrimp with one ounce of ice cold Bloody Mary mix. Float the chilled vodka on top of the Bloody Mary mix, about a half ounce per portion.

Using a fine grater, cover the tops of the glasses with fresh horseradish.

Garnish with the chopped scallion tops and serve ice cold.

***Note:** Preferably "Twisted Spoke" brand.

ABOUT RICK TRAMONTO

www.cenitare.com • www.trurestaurant.com
www.cheftramonto.com

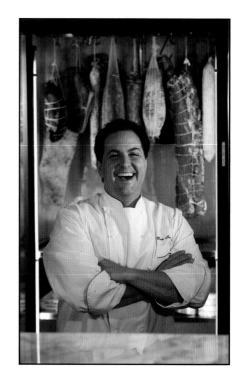

Recognized in 1994 as one of *Food & Wine's* Top Ten Best New Chefs and in 2002 as Best Chef: Midwest Region by The James Beard Foundation, Rick Tramonto has garnered international attention and a host of prestigious awards for his work at Trio, Brasserie T and his renowned four-star, Relais-Gourmand restaurant Tru in Chicago. Tramonto has a history of television work, including *Oprah, Today, CBS This Morning* and the TV Food Network.   His sixth cookbook, *Fantastico!* is a tour of Italy one small plate at a time and will be released in autumn 2007. In 2006 he founded Cenitare Restaurants with culinary partner Gale Gand, a restaurant management and development company which opened four new concepts: The Westin Chicago North Shore, including Tramonto's Steak & Seafood, Osteria di Tramonto, and RT Lounge.

Q: If you could meet Auguste Escoffier, what would you ask him?
A: What were his inspirations and how did he come up with such genius flavor combinations and such beautiful dishes without the aid of modern kitchen tools?

Q: If you were condemned to die, what would be your last meal?
A: White Truffle Risotto.

Q: What food could you live without and why?
A: Fruitcake. Why? Doesn't it answer itself?

Q: Was your mother a good cook? What is your mother's best dish and can you duplicate it?
A: Yes. Lasagne, and it is on the menu at Osteria di Tramonto named "Gloria's Lasagne."

SHRIMP COCKTAIL

PAN-FRIED OYSTERS
WITH GINGER CRÈME FRAÎCHE
AND PEPPERS

PAN-FRIED OYSTERS WITH GINGER CRÈME FRAÎCHE AND PEPPERS

BY CAPRIAL & JOHN PENCE • SERVES 6

3 MULTI COLORED SWEET PEPPERS,
   JULIENNED
1 TABLESPOON EXTRA VIRGIN OLIVE
   OIL
   SALT AND BLACK PEPPER

GINGER CRÈME FRAÎCHE:
1½ CUPS CRÈME FRAÎCHE
2 TABLESPOONS FRESH GINGER,
   MINCED
1 TEASPOON FRESH CILANTRO,
   CHOPPED
   SALT AND BLACK PEPPER

OYSTERS:
30 FRESH SMALL OYSTERS
2 CUPS FLOUR
1 CUP FINE CORNMEAL
1 PINCH CAYENNE
   SALT AND BLACK PEPPER
2 TABLESPOONS EXTRA VIRGIN
   OLIVE OIL

To prepare the peppers: heat a large sauté pan with oil until hot, add the peppers and lower the heat to medium low. Cook the peppers slowly until very tender, season with salt and black pepper. Keep warm or room temperature.

To prepare the crème fraîche: place the crème in a bowl and add the ginger and cilantro, mix well. Season with salt and black pepper, keep cold until ready to use.

To prepare the oysters: combine the flour, cornmeal, cayenne, salt, and pepper in a bowl and mix well. Dredge the oysters in the flour mixture and set aside. Heat a very large sauté pan until very hot, add the oil and heat until smoking hot. Add the oysters and cook until crispy on both sides. Drain on paper towels.

On six plates place a bit of the peppers then five of the oysters, top with crème fraîche. Serve warm.

CAPRIAL'S BISTRO

Q: What put you on the culinary career path?
A: I needed to get out of the house. My parents had had enough of me (John).

Q: If not for food, where would you be now?
A: Struggling as a painter (Caprial).

Q: If you could eat anywhere in the world, where would it be?
A: On a beautiful boat off the coast of southern France, near Cassis (John).

Q: What food could you live without and why?
A: Beets, can't stand anything about them (Caprial).

ABOUT CAPRIAL AND JOHN PENCE

www.caprialandjohnskitchen.com

For the past fourteen years Caprial and John Pence have owned and operated Caprial's Bistro, a restaurant located in a small quaint neighborhood just southeast of downtown Portland Oregon. The Pences share a passion for food that has been cultivated over the years.

The paths that they have traveled to reach the present have, however, been quite different. John and Caprial grew up on opposite coasts. Both gravitated toward cooking. Caprial's passion for cooking was sparked at an early age while John's was fueled by a post graduation restaurant job. Their paths crossed at the Culinary Institute of America where they attended school.

In the mid-eighties, following graduation, the Pences' moved to Seattle, a city that they credit for launching their culinary careers. Experiences combined, they have worked in every size and style restaurant imaginable. Ten years ago Caprial teamed up with the Learning Channel to do a cooking show, *Caprial's Cafe*. Several years later the cooking series moved to Public Television. In 2000, Caprial and John began to do the show together, *Cooking with Caprial & John*. In September of 2003, the Pences' co-produced the most recent series with OPB, *Caprial & John's Kitchen; Cooking for Friends and Family*. The series will air nationally on public television stations. Caprial alone has written eight cookbooks, the most recent was co-authored with John, and assumes the role of the companion book to the *Caprial & John's Kitchen* series, titled *Caprial & John's Kitchen; Recipes for Cooking Together*.

TURK HILL BROILED OYSTERS

BY WHITEY SCHMIDT • SERVES 4

OYSTERS:

24   FRESH OYSTERS, WHOLE

       ROCK SALT

½   CUP CHARDONNAY

SPINACH:

2   CUPS FRESH SPINACH

       SALT AND PEPPER

WHITE SAUCE:

2½   TABLESPOONS BUTTER

2½   TABLESPOONS FLOUR

2   CUPS MILK

       RESERVED OYSTER COOKING

         LIQUID

       SALT

       FRESHLY GRATED NUTMEG

½   CUP FINE, FRESH BREADCRUMBS

½   CUP GRATED GRUYERE CHEESE

Scrub the oysters and shuck them, reserving their deep cupped shells. Set the shells on a baking sheet lined with rock salt. Set aside.

Place the oysters in a sauce pan and pour wine into the sauce pan to cover. Slowly poach oysters for 1 to 2 minutes just until the edges begin to curl.

Remove oysters from wine, reserve both, oysters and cooking liquid, separately

Boil fresh spinach in salted water, drain and chop spinach. Season with salt and pepper and set aside.

In a small saucepan, melt butter, stir in flour. Pour in milk and the reserved oyster poaching liquid. Stir constantly. Add salt and nutmeg. Simmer over medium low heat until thickened. Set aside.

To assemble, evenly cover the bottom of each reserved half shell with cooked spinach and top with one oyster.

Cover the oyster with white sauce and evenly sprinkle with breadcrumbs and cheese.

Broil until golden brown and bubbly.

Garnish with freshly grated nutmeg and serve immediately.

TURK HILL BROILED OYSTERS

ABOUT DAVID MYERS

www.sonarestaurant.com

As co-chef and co-owner of Sona, David's cultural vision is defined by a firm commitment to the finest produce, especially from California's artisan farmers, a respect for the seasons, and a belief in spontaneity. His fluency in classic French traditions and techniques allows him to draw upon multi-cultural flavors with perpetual innovation.

Alongside his wife and co-chef/co-owner of Sona, Michelle Myers, David embodies the Japanese concept of "kappo" which emphasizes capturing the moment when an ingredient is at its freshest and purest.

David's ease in the kitchen has been honed from several years spent fine-tuning his skills in some of the most renowned kitchens in the U.S. and Europe.

Although David headed to college with the intention of studying international business, he discovered food and set out on a path that led him to Charlie Trotter's in Chicago. Chef Trotter sent David to work at Gerard Boyer's 3-Michelin-starred Les Crayeres in Reims, France. After returning to the U.S., David continued his studies under the tutelage of Chef Daniel Boulud at Restaurant Daniel in New York City.

David then joined Chef/Restaurateur Joachim Splichal as executive sous-chef at Patina in Los Angeles where he participated in the renovation and re-opening of the famed restaurant. Shortly thereafter, David joined the executive board of Raffles L'Ermitage Hotel in Beverly Hills where he became executive chef and opened Restaurant JAAN. He also supervised the opening of JAAN at the Westin Stamford Equinox in Singapore.

David has been featured on CNN as well as in the following publications: *Los Angeles Times, Los Angeles Magazine, SOMA, Departures, The Financial Times, Women's Wear Daily, Food and Wine, Gayot Publications, Jay Weston Newsletter* and *Beverly Hills 213*.

David and his wife Michelle live in Los Angeles. David quenches his thirst for culinary and cultural knowledge with constant world travel and periodic visits to Michelin-starred restaurants throughout Europe.

GEODUCK CLAM SASHIMI

Q: What is your favorite comfort food?
A: Any home cooked meal made from scratch.

Q: What put you on the culinary career path?
A: Once I started cooking, it completely took me and I couldn't let go.

Q: If not for food, where would you be now?
A: I'd be rich and surfing.

SONA

OYSTERS WITH PEAS, YOGURT, LEMON, AND ALTOIDS

BY KAT FUKUSHIMA • SERVES 4

A combination of flavors that I love; peas, yogurt, lemon, oyster, and mint. Originally it was a pea soup that I decided to modify. This is the dish that came forth. To me it is a balance of many flavors; salty, briny, sweet, and acidic all packed on a little shell. The Altoids, which to me have the flavor of mint tenfold, substitute for the mint leaves.

⅓   cup Greek yogurt

12   each oysters, shucked, retain liquid and bottom

1   cup frozen peas

     sea salt to taste

1   lemon, cut in half

     Greek olive oil

1   or 2 Altoids, mint flavored

Place a colander over a bowl that is lined with a coffee filter or a few layers of cheesecloth. Place the yogurt in the coffee filter or cheesecloth and place in the refrigerator overnight. Reserve any yogurt water that accrues in the bowl separate from the strained yogurt.

Shuck the oysters retaining any of their liquid. Be careful not to splinter the shells. Carefully inspect the oysters for broken shell pieces. Pour the oyster liquid through a fine mesh strainer and reserve. Wash and dry the reserved bottom shell from the oysters.

Combine the frozen peas, the reserved yogurt water and oyster liquid and put it through a juicer to collect the fresh green water of the peas. Taste and adjust with sea salt.

Assembly: Using an empty egg carton bottom prop the oyster shells so they sit as level as possible. Put one oyster in per shell. Spoon 1 teaspoon of the green pea liquid per oyster. Squeeze a few drops of fresh lemon juice from ½ lemon.

With a Microplane® zester, spank the remaining lemon half over the oysters. In doing so you bring out the natural oils of the lemon along with the zest, sending them flying over the oysters.

With two demitasse spoons place a small quenelle of yogurt on each oyster. Drizzle a few drops of the Greek olive oil on each oyster. Finely grate an Altoid over the oysters.

Serving suggestion: Place oysters on a bed of crushed ice or seaweed, presented on a large serving plate.

ABOUT KAT FUKUSHIMA

www.cafeatlantico.com

As head chef of Café Atlántico, Chef Katsuya Fukushima's charming, playful, and highly personal style of cuisine has surprised and delighted the palate of Washingtonians.

With boundless curiosity and a refusal to let conventions about food be an impediment to creativity, Fukushima has managed to turn his kitchen into one of the most inventive in the country, churning out unexpected delights. Diners can find Fukushima's philosophy in action in the form of the foie gras truffle which asks "why does candy have to be sweet?" Or in the innovative "ravioli" his kitchen produces using paper thin slices of pineapple, jicama, and mango in the place of conventional pasta.

Fukushima was named chef of Café Atlántico in 2002 after a stint at Verbena in New York and after working for a season at the famed el Bulli in Roses, Spain. There Fukushima came under the influence of Master Chef Ferran Adria.

During his career, Fukushima has had the opportunity to cook for some of the most influential chefs in the world including Adria, Thomas Keller, and David Bouley. He has also cooked for a number of dinners at the James Beard House in New York.

Fukushima was recently named "Rising Star" by StarChefs. He has also been nominated several times as "Rising Star" by the Restaurant Association of Metropolitan Washington.

Recently, Fukushima appeared in an episode of *Gourmet's Diary of a Foodie*, cooked in Kitchen Stadium for an episode of *Iron Chef* and will appear in a segment on *Sugar Rush* in early 2007. In addition, he has appeared in a variety of media outlets including the *Washington Post, Washingtonian, Wine Spectator, Food Arts*, and was featured in several episodes of the *Fretz Kitchen*. Smithsonian Resident Associates also featured Fukushima in their popular *Meet the Chef* series.

Fukushima received his formal culinary training at L'Academie de Cuisine where he now teaches a few classes every term. Before deciding on a career in the kitchen, Fukushima attended the University of Maryland where he studied mathematics and art.

Fukushima lives in Washington, DC.

Q: What is your favorite comfort food?
A: My all-time favorite is meatloaf, mashed potatoes and peas. Oh yeah, I need ketchup of course!

Q: If you could eat anywhere in the world, where would it be?
A: I would love to eat at Michel Bras

Q: Was your mother a good cook? What is your mother's best dish and can you duplicate it?
A: Yes, my mom was an awesome cook. She used to make this dish that resembles a Japanese version of a pot au feu, using soy sauce as the main flavoring ingredient. It has chicken, or sometimes beef. Then big pieces of carrots, chunks of potatoes, sometimes sweet potatoes, tied knots of seaweed, gobo, and onions. And of course love. I would not want to make this dish. I want the way mom makes it to be the only way!

OYSTERS WITH PEAS, YOGURT, LEMON, AND ALTOIDS

PORTOBELLO QUESADILLA WITH GRITS

BY NONA NIELSEN-PARKER • SERVES 10

CHIPOTLE LIME CRÈME:

½   CUP SOUR CREAM

1   TEASPOON FINELY CHOPPED
    CHIPOTLE IN ADOBO

½   TEASPOON GRATED LIME ZEST
    SALT AND PEPPER TO TASTE

QUESADILLA MIXTURE:

1   POUND PORTOBELLO
    MUSHROOMS, CUT IN HALF

2   TABLESPOONS VEGETABLE OIL

1   CUP DICED RED ONION

1   TEASPOON GRATED GARLIC

1½ TEASPOON GROUND CUMIN

1   TEASPOON GROUND CORIANDER
    SALT TO TASTE

1   CUP STONE GROUND GRITS,
    COOKED IN 3 CUPS SALTED
    WATER

4   OUNCES BABY SPINACH

¾   CUP GRATED CHEDDAR CHEESE

6   TABLESPOONS SOUR CREAM

1   LIME, ZESTED FINELY

½   CUP ROASTED GRAPE TOMATOES
    TOSSED WITH ¼ TEASPOON
    EACH SALT AND PEPPER (NOTE:
    IF THERE IS NOT ENOUGH TIME
    TO ROAST, JUST CHOP THE SAME
    AMOUNT OF RAW TOMATOES)

10 8-INCH FLOUR TORTILLAS

To prepare the chipotle lime creme: Mix the sour cream, chipotle and lime zest in a small bowl, season to taste and reserve until ready to serve.

To prepare the quesadilla mixture: Slice the halved portobello mushrooms into ⅛-inch crosswise slices.

Heat oil in non stick pan and sauté sliced mushrooms for 5 minutes. Add red onion and sauté another 5 minutes or until both mushrooms and onions are soft. Add garlic, cumin, and coriander and sauté another minute. Taste and add salt if needed. Reserve in bowl.

Meanwhile cook the grits, stirring regularly. When soft and all of the water has been absorbed, add to mushroom mixture. While still warm add spinach, cheese, sour cream, lime zest and roasted tomatoes.

To assemble: Toast tortillas on stove top. Spread quesadilla mixture on one half of the tortilla. Fold over and cut into quarters or smaller. Top with a dollop of chipotle lime crème.

Note: To roast tomatoes: (this can be done up to 2 days ahead) line a sheet pan with parchment, poke a hole in each tomato with a toothpick, toss with salt and pepper, and cook for 1½ hours at 200°.

PORTOBELLO QUESADILLA WITH GRITS

ABOUT MARY SUE MILLIKEN AND SUSAN FENIGER

www.marysueandsusan.com
www.bordergrill.com
www.ciudad-la.com

Mary Sue Milliken and Susan Feniger are two of America's most beloved chefs. The duo have been business partners for over 20 years, beginning with the opening of City Cafe on Melrose Avenue in Los Angeles in 1981. Currently they are hands-on owner-operators of the popular and critically acclaimed Border Grill restaurants in Santa Monica and Las Vegas, serving upscale, modern Mexican food in a hip, urban cantina setting. The pair also own and operate Ciudad restaurant in Downtown Los Angeles, featuring the bold and seductive flavors of the Latin world.

Natural teachers, the partners are prolific in many media outlets. They are authors of five cookbooks, including *Cooking with Too Hot Tamales, Mesa Mexicana,* and *City Cuisine.* They are television veterans, appearing on 396 episodes of the popular "Too Hot Tamales" and "Tamales World Tour" programs on Food Network. Since 1996, they have had several homes on the radio dial in Los Angeles, including KCRW, KFWB, and KFI. In addition, Border Grill and Ciudad dishes "starred" in the 2001 Samuel Goldwyn feature film, *Tortilla Soup.* Mary Sue and Susan are also the creators of the Border Girls brand of fresh prepared foods at Whole Foods Market, as well as a line of signature peppermills and salt mills manufactured by Vic Firth Gourmet.

Mary Sue and Susan are also active members of the community, playing leading roles in many culinary associations and charities, notably Share Our Strength, the Scleroderma Research Foundation, the Chefs Collaborative, and Women Chefs and Restaurateurs.

Q: If not for food, where would you be now?
A: I love science. In my next life I want to be a mad scientist. (Mary Sue)

Q: What is your favorite family recipe?
A: My mom's steak tartar is incredible and we eat it at holidays. (Mary Sue)

Q: If you could eat anywhere in the world, where would it be?
A: India. (Susan)

Q: Was your mother a good cook? What is your mother's best dish and can you duplicate it?
A: My mother was a fantastic cook. She made incredible salads, perfectly seasoned and always with interesting ingredients. Her brisket was pretty yummy too. And yes, I can duplicate her dishes. (Susan)

SPICY BANANA DIP

BRAISED ARTICHOKES (IN THE COUNTRY/ROMAN STYLE) CARCIOFI ALLA ROMANA O IN HUMIDO

BY SUSAN HERMANN-LOOMIS • SERVES 4

This is a rustic, Amalfitana version of this classic Roman dish, which comes from a small vegetable market in the town of Massa Lubrense, on the Amalfi Peninsula. While in Rome the dish is more formal—the artichoke is trimmed, the heart stuffed, the dish intended to be eaten with a knife and fork—here is informal, gutsy.

4	LARGE ARTICHOKES, THE TIPS OF EACH LEAF TRIMMED, RINSED
6	CLOVES GARLIC, GREEN GERM REMOVED
1	LARGE BUNCH FLAT-LEAF PARSLEY, TO GIVE 3 CUPS LEAVES, LOOSELY PACKED
1	PLUS ½ LEMONS FINELY ZESTED
¼	CUP EXTRA-VIRGIN OLIVE OIL
12	SMALL ONIONS, ABOUT THE SIZE OF A GOLF BALL, PEELED AND CUT IN HALF
3	MEDIUM NEW POTATOES (ABOUT 6 OUNCES), PEELED AND CUT INTO 1½-INCH CHUNKS
¼	TO 1 CUP WATER (MAY NEED MORE)
	SEA SALT AND FRESHLY GROUND BLACK PEPPER

Trim off the stems of the artichoke flush with the bottom. Reserve the stems. Turn over the artichoke so the stem end is up, and place it on a hard surface. Press firmly on the artichoke so it flattens slightly, and "opens." Turn the artichokes upright and arrange them in a large stockpot or Dutch oven.

Mince together the garlic and the parsley. Mix the zest of 1 lemon with the garlic and parsley. Open the artichokes enough (if they haven't already opened enough from being pressed) so that you can easily divide the parsley/garlic mixture among them, placing it inside right down to the core of the artichoke. Pour 1 tablespoon oil into each artichoke.

Peel the stems, cut them into ¾-inch lengths, and sprinkle them among the artichokes, along with the onions and the potatoes.

Pour ¼ cup water around the artichokes. Sprinkle with a liberal amount of salt and freshly ground black pepper, cover, and place over medium high heat. When the water comes to a boil, reduce the heat to medium and cook until the artichokes are tender, about 40 minutes. Be prepared to add additional water if necessary. This will depend largely on the type and season of the artichoke—at different times of year they tend to release more water. Check frequently, making sure nothing is burning and sticking to the bottom of the pan. To test for doneness, remove an outer leaf from one of the artichokes, and pierce the heart with a knife. The artichoke leaf and heart should be tender, but not mushy.

To serve, place an artichoke on a warmed plate, and divide the accompanying vegetables among the plates, placing them around the base of the artichoke. Garnish with the zest of the remaining half lemon.

ABOUT SUSAN HERMANN-LOOMIS

www.susanloomis.com

Susan Herrmann Loomis is a France-based, award-winning author with eight books to her credit, a professionally trained chef, and a cooking school proprietor.

Included among her titles are *The Great American Seafood Cookbook, Farmhouse Cookbook, Clambakes and Fish Fries, French Farmhouse Cookbook, Italian Farmhouse Cookbook,* (all Workman Publishing, Inc.) and *On Rue Tatin* (Broadway Books. 2001) a narrative about her life in France, with recipes which won the IACP best literary food book for 2002, *Tarte Tatin* (Harper Collins UK, 2003), the sequel, and *Cooking at Home On Rue Tatin,* (William Morrow, May 2005).

Loomis contributes to many newspapers and magazines including *Cooking Light, Metropolitan Home, The New York Times, Gourmet,* and *Bon Appetit.* Loomis has participated in many television and radio shows, including "Good Morning America" (ABC), "Home Matters," "Epicurious/Discovery," "The Splendid Table with Lynn Rosetto Kasper" (MPR), "Food Talk with Arthur Schwartz" (WOR), "Good Food Hour with Evan Kleinman" (KSRO).

Loomis, who has lived in France for more than fifteen years, operates On Rue Tatin, a cultural and culinary cooking program, from her 15th century home in Louviers, France, where she lives with her two children Joseph and Fiona Rose. Participants spend five delicious days cooking and enjoying the meals they've made along with wines from throughout France, visiting local markets and artisan food producers, and getting an in-depth look at and feeling for all that is wonderful about France. Loomis can be reached at her website, www.onruetatin.com.

ACHIEVEMENTS

- *On Rue Tatin: Cooking in Normandy with Susan Herrmann Loomis,* an exclusive, hands-on cooking and cultural program
- 2005 *Cooking at Home On Rue Tatin* (William Morrow)
- 2001 *On Rue Tatin, Living and Cooking in a French Town* (Broadway Books)

Q: What put you on the culinary career path?

A: My grandmother's lamb shanks, collard greens, and crescent rolls.

Q: If not for food, where would you be now?

A: A professional calligrapher, working in Japan.

Q: What food could you live without and why?

A: I do live without angel food cake, happily. It is, to me, sweet non-substance.

MOM'S CRAB DIP

BY TOM DOUGLAS • ADAPTED FROM HIS BOOK *TOM'S BIG DINNERS* (MORROW, 2003)
SERVES 8

My mom made a delicious creamy crab dip, reminiscent of Thousand Islands dressing, that the whole family loved. I like to serve dollops of crab dip on homemade potato chips, but you can use good-quality purchased potato chips if you prefer.

1	LEMON
3	TABLESPOONS TOMATO PASTE
1	TABLESPOON HONEY
¾	CUP MAYONNAISE, HOMEMADE OR PURCHASED (SUCH AS BEST FOODS)
2	TABLESPOONS THINLY SLICED CHIVES
1	TABLESPOON SEEDED AND MINCED SWEET RED CHERRY PEPPER (FROM A JAR OF VINEGAR-PACKED SWEET CHERRY PEPPERS)
1	TEASPOON PREPARED HORSERADISH
¼	TEASPOON TABASCO
1	HARD-BOILED EGG, FINELY CHOPPED
¾	POUND FRESH DUNGENESS CRABMEAT, PICKED OVER FOR BITS OF SHELL AND CARTILAGE WITH CLAW MEAT AND LARGE PIECES OF CRAB LEFT WHOLE

KOSHER SALT AND FRESHLY GROUND BLACK PEPPER

POTATO CHIPS, HOMEMADE OR TOP QUALITY PURCHASED

Using a fine zester, grate the zest from the lemon, measuring out 2 teaspoons. Cut the lemon in half and squeeze, measuring out 1 tablespoon of juice and removing any seeds. (Reserve the rest of the lemon for seasoning the dip with more juice later.)

Put the lemon zest and juice in a large bowl, add the tomato paste and honey, and whisk together until smooth.

Whisk in the mayonnaise, chives, cherry pepper, horseradish, and Tabasco. Using a rubber spatula, gently fold in the egg.

Add the crabmeat to the bowl and toss it with the dressing. Season to taste with salt and pepper and a little more lemon juice

Serving suggestion: Set a bowl of crab dip on a large platter and surround it with potato chips for dipping.

Suggested wine: Ste. Michelle Riesling (Washington State).

Notes: You can make the dressing a day ahead and store it, covered and refrigerated. When you're ready to serve, mix the crabmeat with the dressing.

Feel free to substitute whichever local crabmeat (such as Blue Crab) is fresh in your area for the Dungeness called for in the recipe.

Since the crab dip is rich and creamy, follow it with something roasted or grilled, such as grilled salmon.

ABOUT TOM DOUGLAS

www.tomdouglas.com

Tom Douglas, along with his wife and business partner, Jackie Cross, owns five of Seattle's most exciting restaurants: Dahlia Lounge (nominated for Best Restaurant by the James Beard Association in 2006), Etta's, Palace Kitchen (nominated for Best New Restaurant by the James Beard Association in 1997), Lola, and Serious Pie. In addition, Tom runs a retail bakery, Dahlia Bakery, a catering business, Tom Douglas' Catering and Events, and an event space, Palace Ballroom. All of Tom's restaurants are located in downtown Seattle.

Over the course of more than 20 years, Tom has been featured as the Seattle chef who has helped to define the Northwest Style. Tom's creativity with local ingredients and his respect for Seattle's ethnic traditions have helped him win numerous awards and accolades including the James Beard Award for Best Northwest Chef in 1994.

Tom's love of food continues to evolve beyond the restaurant scene. He is the author of three cookbooks, *Tom Douglas' Seattle Kitchen* (Morrow, 2001), which won a James Beard award for Best Americana Cookbook, *Tom's Big Dinners* (Morrow, 2003), and *I Love Crab Cakes* (Morrow, 2006). In addition, Tom's specialty food line, which includes Rub with Love spice rubs plus barbecue and teriyaki sauces, is sold nationwide. Tom also hosts his own weekly talk radio show, "Tom Douglas' Seattle Kitchen," on 710 KIRO.

Tom lives in Seattle, Washington, with his wife, Jackie, and daughter, Loretta.

Q: If you were condemned to die, what would be your last meal?
A: 5-Spice Duck with Green Onion Pancakes and Hoisin Sauce.

Q: If you could eat anywhere in the world, where would it be?
A: L'Ami Louis in Paris.

Q: What is your favorite family recipe?
A: Mom's Crab Dip.

PARMESAN POPS

BY DAN BARBER • MAKES 24 POPS

1	TABLESPOON CHOPPED FRESH PARSLEY
1	TABLESPOON CHOPPED FRESH TARRAGON
1	TABLESPOON CHOPPED FRESH CHERVIL OR OTHER HERB FROM YOUR GARDEN
1	LEMON, FINELY ZESTED
2	CUPS FINELY GRATED PARMESAN CHEESE
24	EACH 8-INCH BAMBOO SKEWERS

Preheat the oven to 350°.

Place a silpat on a baking sheet.

Mix herbs and zest in a small bowl.

Place 1 full teaspoon mound of cheese on the silpat down the long side of the sheet pan, alternating opposite sides of the pan and leaving about 1½ inches between each. That will allow room for the cheese to spread.

Place the pointed end of the skewer on top of each mound of cheese. Place the baking sheet into the oven and bake for 8 to 10 minutes or until the cheese has melted, is golden brown and bubbling.

Remove from the oven and sprinkle each circle of cheese with a mix of herbs while the cheese is still hot.

When cool, remove each pop from the silpat with a small offset spatula.

Note: Depending on your sheet pan size, you will need between 2 to 3 trays.

Q: If you could meet Auguste Escoffier, what would you ask him?
A: When did you find time to write the book?

Q: What is your favorite family recipe?
A: I have two: my father's scrambled eggs and my aunt's scrambled eggs. My father's were rubbery, at best, but more often burnt, dry, and flakey. I ate them all the time as a kid (breakfast, lunch, dinner). And then one day, in the midst of a bout of strep throat, my aunt made me scrambled eggs, whisked over a double boiler, finished with pounds of butter and herbs. I still remember how they slid down my throat. But looking back on it now, I realize I couldn't have had one without the other—my dad's eggs made me appreciate my aunt's.

ABOUT DAN BARBER

www.bluehillstonebarns.com

Since May 2000, Dan has seen Blue Hill grow from a noted neighborhood restaurant to most recently receiving a 3-star *New York Times* review. In the summer of 2002, *Food and Wine Magazine* featured Dan as one of the country's "Best New Chefs." He has since addressed food system issues through op-eds in the *New York Times*. In addition, his writing has been featured in "Best Food Writing 2004," "Best Food Writing 2005," and "Best Food Writing 2006."

Blue Hill at Stone Barns and Stone Barns Center for Food and Agriculture opened their doors in 2004. As the restaurant's chef/owner and the center's creative director, Dan helped create the philosophical and practical framework for Stone Barns Center for Food and Agriculture and continues to help guide it in its mission to create a consciousness about the effects of everyday food choices. Frank Bruni of the *New York Times* awarded Blue Hill at Stone Barns 3 stars.

Both Blue Hill and Blue Hill at Stone Barns have received Best New Restaurant nominations from the James Beard Foundation. In the spring of 2006, Dan was awarded Best Chef: New York City.

Dan serves on Harvard's Center for Health and the Global Environment advisory board. He has been working with likeminded organizations to minimize the political and intellectual rhetoric around agricultural policies and to instead maximize the appreciation of eating good food.

ACHIEVEMENTS

* 2006 James Beard Award: Best Chef, NYC
* 2002 *Food & Wine* Magazine: Best New Chef
* *New York Times* 3-Star review, Blue Hill New York & Blue Hill at Stone Barns

BLUE HILL AT STONE BARNS

PHOTOGRAPH BY CARINA SALVI

HERB-ROLLED PAPPARDELLE WITH LEMON BROWN BUTTER

BY JOANNE WEIR • SERVES 4

1	CUP ALL-PURPOSE FLOUR
1/8	TEASPOON SALT
1	EGG
3/4	CUP LOOSELY PACKED MIXTURE OF HERBS: FLAT-LEAF PARSLEY, SAGE, OREGANO, BASIL, MINT, STEMS REMOVED COMPLETELY
5	TABLESPOONS UNSALTED BUTTER
1	TABLESPOON FINELY GRATED LEMON ZEST
1	TEASPOON LEMON JUICE
3/4	CUP GRATED PARMIGIANO-REGGIANO AS A GARNISH

In the bowl of a food processor, pulse together the flour and salt. Add the egg and 1 tablespoon water and process until the dough forms a soft ball but is not sticky. If it is sticky, add more flour a tablespoon at a time until it is no longer sticky. Remove the dough and wrap in plastic. Let the dough rest at room temperature for 30 minutes or overnight in the refrigerator.

Divide the pasta dough into 3 pieces. With a pasta machine, roll one piece of the pasta out to 1/8-inch thick. Place the sheet of pasta flat on the work surface. Place the herbs in a single layer on top of half of the length of the sheet of pasta. Spray the pasta and herbs lightly with a mist of water. Fold the other half of the sheet of pasta over the herbs and press together. Roll the pasta once again through the pasta machine until it is 1/16-inch thick. Using a scalloped pastry cutter, cut the pasta across into 1-inch wide strips called pappardelle. Dust lightly with flour and tap off the excess. Place a kitchen towel on a baking sheet and dust with flour. Place the pasta on the towel. Continue with the remaining 2 pieces of pasta.

In the meantime, melt the butter in a saucepan over medium high heat. Cook the butter until the butter solids turn golden brown and it just begins to smoke, 3 to 4 minutes. Add the lemon zest, lemon juice, salt and pepper. Turn off the heat.

Bring a large pot of salted water to a boil over high heat. Add the pappardelle and simmer until the pasta is tender 1 to 2 minutes. Drain and toss with the lemon brown butter. To serve, place on a warm platter and sprinkle with Parmigiano.

Serving suggestion: I prefer to serve pasta like the Italians as a first course.

Notes: Advanced preparation, storage, and freezing: Make the papparadelle a day in advance. After the papparadelle has been rolled and cut, spread it out on a baking sheet lined with a kitchen towel which has been dusted with flour and either dry it at room temperature on the counter or place it in the refrigerator. Or make it several days in advance and freeze the papparadelle.

Special equipment: Pasta machine, zigzag pasta roller.

Recommended wine: Chardonnay.

HERB-ROLLED PAPPARDELLE
WITH LEMON BROWN BUTTER

ABOUT SUSAN SPICER

www.bayona.com

Susan Spicer began her cooking career in New Orleans at the Louis XVI Restaurant in 1979. After a 4-month "stage" at the Hotel Sofitel in Paris in 1982, she returned to New Orleans to open the Savoir Faire as Chef de Cuisine. In 1985, she traveled extensively, returning to New Orleans to work at Henri.

In 1986 she opened Bistro at Maison de Ville. After nearly four years as chef, she formed a partnership with Regina Keever and in the spring of 1990 opened Bayona in a beautiful, 200-year-old cottage in the French Quarter. Bayona soon earned national attention and has been featured in *Food and Wine, Gourmet, Food Arts, Travel & Leisure, Bon Appetit* and *The New York Times*.

From 1997 through 1999, Susan owned and operated Spice, Inc., a specialty food market with take-out food, cooking classes and artisan bakery. This developed into Wild Flour Breads, which she currently co-owns with partner Sandy Whann.

In 2000, Susan and three partners opened Herbsaint in the Warehouse District of New Orleans.

In 2001, as consulting chef, Susan opened Cobalt, a regional American restaurant in the Hotel Monaco, owned by the Kimpton Group of San Francisco.

Susan also contributes to numerous charity events including Share Our Strength's annual "Taste of the Nation" in New Orleans and the Superbowl hunger-relief fundraiser "Taste of the NFL."

Susan is currently working on her first cookbook, which will be out in the fall of 2007. In New Orleans, she can be found in the kitchen at either Bayona or Herbsaint most nights of the week.

ACHIEVEMENTS

- For the last three years, *Gourmet's* Readers' Poll "Top 5 Restaurants" in New Orleans
- 1998 Nation's Restaurant News "Fine Dining Hall of Fame"
- 1996 Restaurants and Institutions "Ivy Award"
- 1995 Mondavi "Culinary Excellence Award"
- 1993 James Beard Award for "Best Chef, Southeast Region"

Q: What is your favorite comfort food?
A: Ice Cream.

Q: If you could eat anywhere in the world, where would it be?
A: Thailand.

Q: What is your favorite family recipe?
A: Pork sates with peanut sauce.

LEMONGRASS SCALLOPS WITH ROASTED PINEAPPLE RELISH

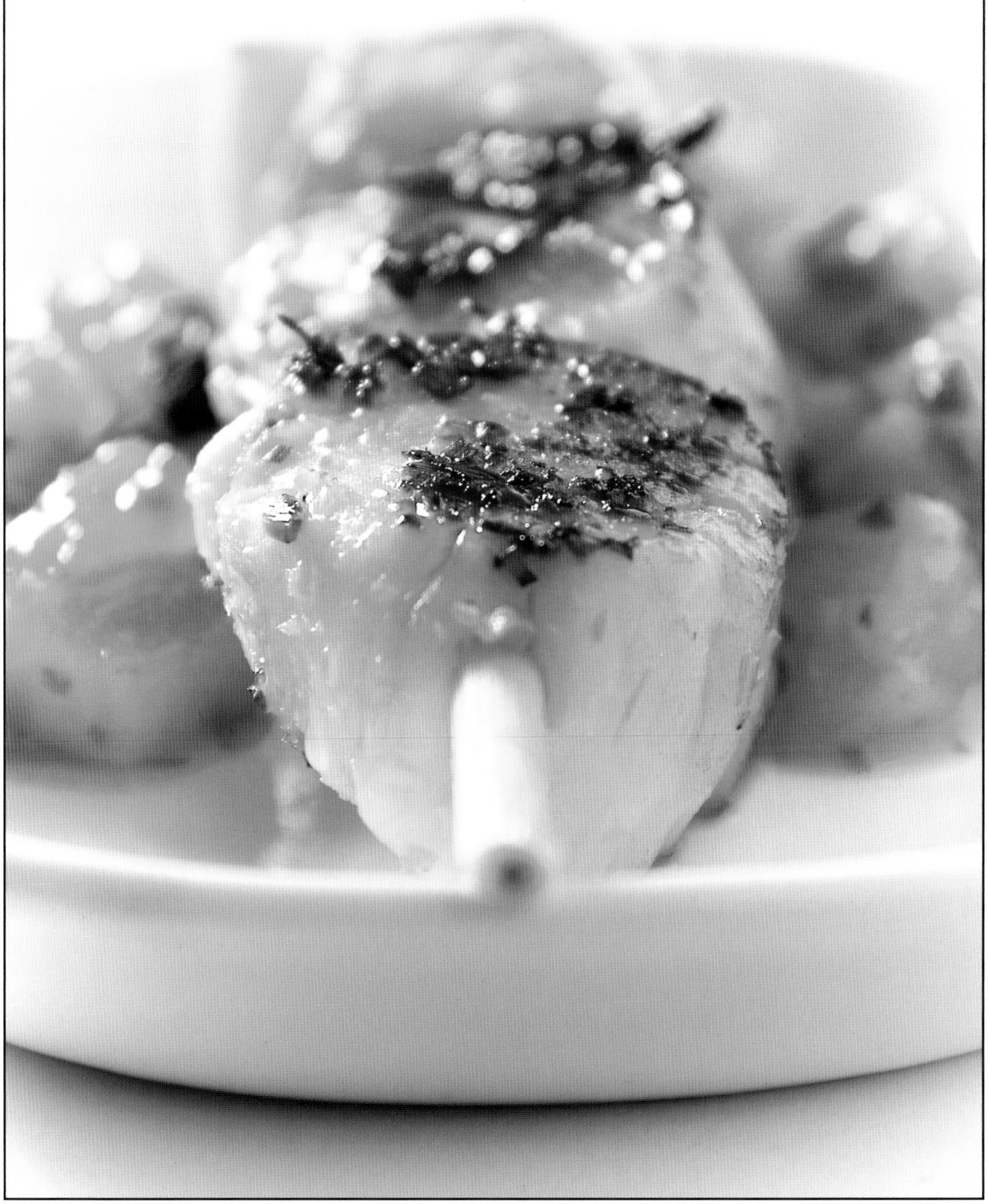

WILD CAUGHT SPOT PRAWNS WITH BUTTERNUT SQUASH SLAW AND BLOOD ORANGE

BY HELENE KENNAN • SERVES 6

1	MEDIUM TO LARGE BUTTERNUT SQUASH
2	PLUS 1 BLOOD ORANGES
¼	CUP WHITE BALSAMIC VINEGAR
¼	CUP PLUS 1 TABLESPOON AVOCADO OIL OR OLIVE OIL
1	CUP FRESH BASIL
¼	TEASPOON FRESH GRATED CINNAMON
¼	TEASPOON FRESH GRATED NUTMEG
¼	TEASPOON FRESH GRATED GINGER
	SALT AND PEPPER TO TASTE
1	POUND WILD-CAUGHT SPOT PRAWNS, PEELED, DEVEINED
6	TO 8 LARGE PECANS

For the slaw: Place 3 cups of water in medium saucepan over high heat. Bring water to boil. Peel, seed and grate butternut squash. Blanch the squash in boiling water for 1 minute. Drain well and spread out on a sheet pan to cool.

Segment 2 blood oranges and reserve any juice that might accumulate during this process in a separate bowl. Juice the remaining blood orange into the bowl with the reserved juice.

In a small mixing bowl, whisk together the white balsamic vinegar, blood orange juice and ¼ cup avocado oil or olive oil. Add cinnamon, nutmeg, ginger, salt and pepper. Set aside ¼ cup of this dressing.

In a medium non-aluminum mixing bowl, combine squash and dressing minus the ¼ cup set aside. Allow to sit for at least 20 minutes so flavors meld properly.

For the shrimp: Place a large sauté pan over medium high heat and add a tablespoon of avocado oil or olive oil. Season the prawns with salt and pepper. Add prawns to hot pan and sauté until just cooked through.

To assemble: As the prawns are cooking add blood orange segments and basil to squash and place a small amount of the slaw in the center of each plate. Place prawns just off the side of the slaw and drizzle a small mount of ¼ cup of reserved dressing over the prawns and the plate.

Grate the pecans over the plates.

Chef's tip: Don't limit yourself to just the prawns. Think sautéed soft shell crabs or crispy duck breast.

ABOUT HELENE KENNAN

www.bamco.com • www.womenchefs.org

In her role as Executive Chef for Bon Appétit Management Co. at the Getty Center, Helene Kennan brings dedication, inventiveness and professionalism of her craft to the table. Overseeing a multi-million dollar food operation, Helene is devoted to training and developing her staff, utilizing sustainable, seasonal and organic ingredients, and bringing world class food to one of Los Angeles' leading cultural institutions.

Helene is president of Women Chefs and Restaurateurs (WCR), a 2500 member trade organization dedicated to the advancement of women in the restaurant industry. Kennan, along with a passionate board of directors, administers and guide programs to prepare women for executive level positions in hospitality. WCR offers mentorship, professional networking and a highly successful scholarship program for women at all stages of their careers.

Q: If you were condemned to die, what would be your last meal?

A: I would request a Philly cheesesteak from Rose Tree Steaks in Media, Pennsylvania. I don't even know if this business still exists but when I was growing up they made the best steak sandwich. It was made with a delicious hoagie roll, thin crispy crust on the outside with an airy quality to the inside. The meat was always piping hot coated with white American cheese and littered with grilled onions and sweet peppers. I could leave this world happy after feasting on one of those again.

Q: If not for food where would you be now?

A: I have always said if I was not a chef, I would be an archaeologist, probably on a dig in South America or Africa. Ancient cultures have always fascinated me. Creating the food at The Getty Villa married both of these interests. I was able to research Greek, Roman and Etruscan recipes and integrate them into menu for the modern palette.

Brunch

HONEY-ORANGE PANCAKES

HONEY-ORANGE PANCAKES

BY DORIE GREENSPAN · YIELD: APPROXIMATELY 14 3½ INCH PANCAKES

1	ORANGE
1¼	CUPS ALL-PURPOSE FLOUR
1 ¼	TEASPOONS BAKING POWDER
¼	TEASPOON BAKING SODA
⅛	TEASPOON SALT
1	CUP PLAIN YOGURT
½	CUP FRESH ORANGE JUICE
1	LARGE EGG
⅓	CUP HONEY
3	TABLESPOONS UNSALTED BUTTER, MELTED
⅛	TEASPOON PURE LEMON EXTRACT
	BUTTER, OIL, OR COOKING SPRAY

ORANGE BUTTER (SEE PAGE 263)

Finely zest the rind of the orange; reserve the orange for juicing.

In a medium bowl, whisk together the flour, baking powder, baking soda and salt. In another bowl, whisk together the yogurt, orange juice, egg, honey, melted butter and lemon extract until blended thoroughly.

Pour the liquid ingredients over the dry ingredients and, using the whisk, mix just until everything is combined. (If the batter is lumpy, don't worry.) Switch to a spatula and gently fold in the grated orange zest.

If necessary, lightly butter, oil or spray your griddle or skillet. Preheat the griddle or skillet over medium heat or, if you've got an electric griddle, set it to 350°.

Spoon ¼ cup of batter onto the griddle for each pancake, allowing space for spreading. When the undersides of the pancakes are golden and the tops are speckled with bubbles that pop and stay open, flip the pancakes over with a wide spatula and cook until the other sides are light brown.

Serve with pure maple syrup and Orange Butter (see page 263).

Notes: To keep the pancakes warm (for up to 20 minutes), keep them, lightly covered, on a lined baking sheet in a 200° oven.

When cool, the pancakes can be wrapped airtight (put a piece of wax paper between each pancake), frozen and reheated in a 350° oven, a toaster-oven, or an ordinary pop-up toaster.

ABOUT DORIE GREENSPAN

Called "a culinary guru" by *The New York Times*, Dorie Greenspan is the award-winning author of nine cookbooks and a special correspondent for *Bon Appetit* magazine. Her cookbooks include the bestseller, *Baking with Julia*, the book that accompanied Julia Child's critically-acclaimed television series; *Desserts by Pierre Herme*, for which she introduced, translated and adapted the recipes of the celebrated French pastry chef for Americans; *The Café Boulud Cookbook*, a collection of reminiscences and French-

American recipes from the renowned New York City chef Daniel Boulud; *Chocolate Desserts by Pierre Herme*; *Paris Sweets, Great Desserts from the City's Best Pastry Shops*; and, most recently, *Baking, From My Home to Yours*, which was named one of the top 50 books of 2006 by amazon.com and chosen as 2006's favorite cookbook by jessicasbiscuit.com. For *Baking with Julia*, Dorie received both a James Beard Foundation Award and an award from the International Association of Culinary Professionals (IACP), while *Desserts by Pierre Herme* was named the IACP Cookbook of the Year. *Chocolate Desserts by Pierre Herme* won the Gourmand World Cookbook Award for "Best Book in All Categories" in the English language and the Mazille Prize for International Cookbook of the Year; and *Paris Sweets* was nominated for a James Beard Foundation Award.

As a food writer, Dorie won a James Beard Foundation Journalism Award for her *Bon Appetit* article, "How French Women Bake". She has been featured often in *The New York Times* and is the restaurant critic for the Louis Vuitton City Guide to New York.

Dorie lives in New York City, Westbrook, Connecticut and Paris.

Q: What is your favorite comfort food?

A: I've got many—make that many, many—comfort foods. My favorite hot comfort food is rice and my favorite cold comfort food is ice cream.

Q: What put you on the culinary career path?

A: Marriage. When I got married, I was a virgin cook—I'd never even made a chocolate-chip cookie, let alone a meal—but I had to cook and wanted to learn to do it well. Once I got started there was no stopping. It was husband, Michael, who encouraged me to make food, which had become my passion, my profession.

Q: Was your mother a good cook? What is your mother's best dish and can you duplicate it?

A: Mom a good cook? Not only wasn't my mom a good cook, she wasn't a cook. She loved good food, she just didn't want to be the one to make it, and so she didn't. She did, however, make memorable crab-salad sandwiches, which I can duplicate with one exception: I can't duplicate the fun we had standing at the kitchen counter laughing over the messy job of cleaning the crab.

GRUYERE AND BACON TART

BY NICK MALGIERI • SERVES 10

Perfect for brunch or lunch, this tart is a distant cousin of both French quiche and a traditional breakfast tart served during Carnival at Basel in Switzerland. Make sure to use real Swiss Gruyere for the filling, or the tart won't have much flavor.

PASTRY DOUGH

1¾ CUPS ALL-PURPOSE FLOUR
    (SPOON FLOUR INTO
    DRY-MEASURE CUP AND LEVEL
    OFF)
1 TEASPOON SALT
1 TEASPOON BAKING POWDER
10 TABLESPOONS UNSALTED BUTTER
    (1¼ STICKS) COLD, CUT INTO
    8 OR 10 PIECES
5 TABLESPOONS COLD WATER

CHEESE FILLING

4 OUNCES BACON, CUT INTO
    ¼-INCH PIECES
2 CUPS SWISS GRUYERE (ABOUT
    6 OUNCES) COARSELY GRATED
3 TABLESPOONS ALL-PURPOSE
    FLOUR
1¾ CUPS HEAVY WHIPPING CREAM
    OR HALF AND HALF
4 LARGE EGGS
¼ TEASPOON SALT
⅛ TEASPOON FRESHLY GRATED
    NUTMEG

1 11- OR 12-INCH TART PAN WITH
    REMOVABLE BOTTOM

For the dough, combine the flour, salt, and baking powder in the bowl of a food processor fitted with the metal blade and pulse several times to mix. Add the butter and pulse until the butter is in ¼- to ⅛-inch pieces. Add the water and pulse until the dough forms a ball. Invert the dough to a floured work surface, carefully remove the blade, and form it into a thick disk.

Flour the dough and roll it to a 14-inch disk. Fold the dough in half and transfer it to the pan, lining up the fold with the diameter of the pan. Unfold the dough into the pan and press it well into the bottom and side of the pan. Use a bench scraper or the back of a knife to sever the excess dough at the rim of the pan. Chill the crust while preparing the filling.

Set a rack in the lowest level of the oven and preheat to 375°.

Cook the bacon over low heat in a small sauté pan until it is crisp. Use a slotted spoon to remove it from the fat and drain the bacon on paper towels. Cool the bacon and evenly scatter it on the crust.

Toss the cheese with the flour and evenly distribute it on the pastry crust. Whisk the remaining ingredients together and pour over the cheese.

Bake the tart until the crust is baked through and the filling is set and well colored, about 30 minutes.

Cool the tart to lukewarm in the pan on a rack.

Serve the tart warm or at room temperature. For advance preparation, make the crust up to a day in advance, wrap and chill it. Cook the bacon and get the other ingredients ready early in the day, but bake the tart no more than an hour or two before you plan to serve it.

ABOUT NICK MALGIERI
www.nickmalgieri.com

Nick Malgieri, former Executive Pastry Chef at Windows on the World, is a 1996 inductee into Who's Who of Food and Beverage in America. He is the author of countless acclaimed cookbooks, receiving top honors from culinary organizations around the world.

A graduate of the Culinary Institute of America, he apprenticed in Switzerland, was subsequently employed at the Hotel de Paris, the Sporting Club in Monte Carlo and the Reserve de Beaulieu in France. In New York, he was Assistant Pastry Chef at the Waldorf Astoria; Executive Chef at Paine Webber, Inc.; and Pastry Chef at the Board Room, a private club.

Malgieri began teaching in the New School Culinary Arts Program in 1979 and, in 1981, became chairman of its Baking Department. He developed and taught the professional baking curriculum for the New York Restaurant School and authored the baking section of its textbook. As founder and owner of the Total Heaven Baking Company, Malgieri also consults to restaurants and pastry shops throughout the United States.

Malgieri's recipes have been published in the *New York Times*, *Family Circle*, *Ladies' Home Journal*, and countless other publications. His writing has appeared in the *New York Daily News*, *Gourmet*, *Chocolatier*, *Food & Wine*, and *Cook's Illustrated*. His monthly column, "Ask the Baker," is syndicated throughout the United States.

Since 1985, he has appeared on local and national television and at culinary events throughout North America, including the Smithsonian Institution.

Currently, Malgieri directs the baking program at the Institute of Culinary Education (formerly Peter Kump's New York Cooking School) and makes guest appearances at many other cooking schools.

ACHIEVEMENTS

• 2006 *Perfect Light Desserts* (Morrow)
• 2005 *A Baker's Tour* (HarperCollins)
• 2002 *Perfect Cakes* (HarperCollins)

Q: If you could meet Auguste Escoffier, what would you ask him?
A: If I could meet Auguste Escoffier I would wait for him to ask me a question; one shouldn't annoy a genius with stupid questions.

Q: If you were condemned to die, what would be your last meal?
A: If I were condemned to die I don't think I would be in the mood to eat.

Q: If you could eat anywhere in the world, where would it be?
A: If I could eat anywhere, I would go back to Bangkok right away and eat everything in sight.

GRUYERE AND BACON TART

Q: What is your favorite family recipe?

A: I come from a family where cooking was taken very seriously—I have about a hundred favorite family recipes. If I had to select a few, they might be: Cavatelli with Spicy Tomato Sauce, incorporating a kind of mint called pennyroyal (Menta pulegium), a specialty of my mother's home town in Southern Italy; or my maternal grandmother's Torta di Ricotta, made only for Easter; or my paternal grandmother's Arancini, Sicilian rice balls; or my mother's Sunday Meat Sauce for pasta.

EGG A LA FOLIE

BY ROLAND PASSOT • SERVES 12

Not only is this recipe about the wonderful combination of eggs and truffles, it is about the presentation of the eggs back in their shell. This will make an elegant brunch presentation.

1	DOZEN EGGS (RESERVE THE EGG CARTON)
4	OUNCES UNSALTED BUTTER
	SALT AND BLACK PEPPER TO TASTE
¼	CUP CREAM
1	TABLESPOONS WHITE OR BLACK TRUFFLES, FINELY GRATED (APPROXIMATELY ¼ TO ½ OUNCE)
1	TABLESPOONS TRUFFLE OIL
	CHIVE STICKS FOR GARNISH

To prepare the egg shells: Hold the egg in your hand with the narrower part of the egg upright and extended above your fingers. You are going to want to take the tip portion off. Cut approximate ¼ inch with a light whack with a sharp knife. Discard the lid - reserve the bottom.

Pour the egg content into a large bowl. Rinse the inside of the shells under warm water to clean of inner membrane. Carefully pull any remaining membrane downward to discard.

Cut the opening of the eggs with a scissors to make sure you get a smooth opening that can be refilled easily with a teaspoon.

Drain the eggshells upside down in the carton to dry. When completely dry, turn the shells upright so they can be filled with the egg mixture.

To prepare the eggs: Melt butter in a saucepan over low heat.

Beat eggs until fluffy. Add salt and pepper. Add to the saucepan and let cook over low heat for about 5 to 10 minutes, stirring constantly with a wooden spoon, gently, not vigorously.

Cook the eggs until soft and creamy but not quite set. Add the truffles and truffle oil at the end of the cooking process. Take off the heat. The finished consistency should be that of a soft scrambled egg.

To stop the cooking, add the cream. Correct seasoning to taste.

Alternatively, you may blend in a Cuisinart for a smoother consistency.

Fill the eggshells three-fourths of the way full with the egg mixture and place in an egg cup. If you do not have an egg cup, you can present them on a salt bed or in a painted (ie: black or gold) egg carton. Garnish with a chive stick .

Serving suggestion: Serve with brioche toast and/or toasted country bread.

EGG A LA FOLIE

LA FOLIE

Q: What is your favorite comfort food?

A: My favorite comfort food is Tete de Veau "Ravigote," meat from a whole boiled calf's head, served with a pungent sauce of herbs, anchovies, capers and gherkins.

Q: If you could meet Auguste Escoffier, what would you ask him?

A: I would ask Auguste Escoffier how he thinks he is still influencing cooking and chefs today.

Q: If you were condemned to die, what would be your last meal?

A: My last meal would be champagne with caviar, a good ribeye steak with a great Burgundy wine, and, of course, cheese.

ABOUT ROLAND PASSOT
www.lafolie.com

Chef Roland Passot began his culinary career at the tender age of fifteen in France's gastronomic capital of Lyon. Traditionally trained by some of the most famous chefs in France, he began as an apprentice before working his way up to the position of assistant sous-chef under Chef Paul Lacombe.

At age 20, Passot spent four years in Chicago. In 1981, he became the opening chef at French Room at the Adolphus Hotel in Dallas. While at the French Room, Passot received national accolades and prepared dinners for celebrities and royalty from around the world including Prince Charles and Bob Hope. Following his heart to San Francisco, Passot became the chef at Chez Michel, but it was not meant to be; the restaurant closed soon after he arrived.

Instead of looking for just another place to work Passot, with his wife Jamie opened La Folie in March of 1988. Through his rigorous French training and several positions in the Midwest, Southwest and in San Francisco, Passot had developed his personal style of cooking, in which he showcases at La Folie.

In 1994, Passot teamed up with Edward N. Levine, CEO of Vine Dining Enterprises, Inc. and President of Vine Solutions to develop and open Left Bank in Larkspur, followed by 4 others throughout the Bay Area. These 200 seat brasseries feature "Cuisine Grand-mere," Passot's version of French home-style cooking.

ACHIEVEMENTS:

- 2006 Michelin Guide 1 star
- 2006 James Beard nomination: Best Chef/California
- 2006 Top 100 Fastest Growing Companies (Left Bank), *SF Business Weekly*
- 2006 Top 100 Restaurants (La Folie), *SF Chronicle*
- 2006 Best French Restaurant, *San Francisco Magazine*

HOT POTATO PANCAKES WITH SMOKED SALMON, PICKLED CUCUMBER, AND LEMON CRÈME FRAÎCHE

BY ANNIE WAYTE • SERVES 4

Try this dish for brunch or as a first course to a more elaborate dinner with a glass of pink champagne! Choose good quality smoked salmon from a reputable store. You can make the pancakes a few hours ahead of schedule and warm them in the oven when required. The pickling liquid for the cucumber can be made in advance and will keep well in a sealed jar in the refrigerator for up to one month.

½   CUP UNSEASONED RICE VINEGAR

3   TABLESPOONS SUGAR

2   TEASPOONS CORIANDER SEEDS

1   ENGLISH CUCUMBER, PEELED

1   TABLESPOON PLUS 1 TABLESPOON
     FINELY CHOPPED FRESH DILL
     SEA SALT AND FRESHLY GROUND
     PEPPER TO TASTE

1   POUND RUSSET/IDAHO POTATOES,
     WASHED WITH SKIN ON

1   EGG, BEATEN

½   CUP FINELY DICED ONION

1   TEASPOON FENNEL SEEDS,
     TOASTED AND COARSELY
     CRUSHED

2   TABLESPOONS PLUS 2 TABLE-
     SPOONS OLIVE OIL OR
     CLARIFIED BUTTER

1   LEMON, FINELY ZESTED

¾   CUP CRÈME FRAÎCHE

12   SLICES SMOKED SALMON

1   BUNCH WATERCRESS, TRIMMED

4   CAPERBERRIES, CUT IN HALVES

1   LEMON, CUT INTO 4 WEDGES

Preheat the oven to 375°.

To make the pickling liquid, combine the rice vinegar, sugar and coriander seeds in a saucepan and bring to a boil. Reduce the heat and simmer until the mixture has the consistency of thin syrup, 6-8 minutes. Remove the pan from the heat and allow the syrup to cool completely.

Slice the cucumber into long ribbons on a slicer or with a vegetable peeler, avoiding the seeded core. Place the ribbons in a glass or plastic mixing bowl and combine with the cooled pickling liquid and 1 tablespoon of the chopped dill. Season with sea salt and pepper to taste. Cover with plastic wrap and keep in the refrigerator until required.

Grate the potatoes extra course and place in the center of a clean, dry dishtowel. Fold over the edges, enclosing the potato, and squeeze tight to remove the excess liquid from the potatoes. Place the potato into a large mixing bowl and add the beaten egg, finely diced onion, crushed fennel seeds and the remaining chopped dill and mix thoroughly. Season with a generous pinch of sea salt and pepper.

Heat 1 to 2 tablespoons of the olive oil or clarified butter in a large frying pan on a medium high heat. Divide the potato mixture into 4 equal amounts and spoon into the frying pan forming round pancakes, each approximately 4 inches in diameter. You may need to do this in two batches using the remaining olive oil or clarified butter as needed. Lower the heat to medium and cook until the bottom side of each pancake is golden brown and crispy. Flip the pancakes over with a spatula and continue to cook until the other side is golden brown and crispy. Place into the pre-heated oven until the potato is cooked through, approximately 5 to 6 minutes.

While the pancakes are in the oven stir the lemon zest into the crème fraiche.

To serve, place the hot potato pancakes onto 4 serving plates. Arrange the sliced smoked salmon over one half of each pancake and spoon the crème fraiche onto the other half. Arrange a plume of watercress and a small pile of the pickled cucumber on each plate and garnish with the caperberries and lemon wedge.

HOT POTATO PANCAKES WITH SMOKED SALMON, PICKLED CUCUMBER, AND LEMON CREME FRAICHE

ABOUT ANNIE WAYTE

Annie Wayte began her professional cooking career in the haute cuisine kitchen of London's Mirabelle. She went on to work as a chef at the Michelin-starred Rue St. Jacques and at London's renowned Clarke's.

In 1994, Annie opened Nicole's on London's Bond Street and replicated it in 1999 in New York City. She launched the trendy Notting Hill Café 202, a New York version of which opened in May 2005. She divides her time between London and New York.

ACHIEVEMENTS

• 2006 *Keep It Seasonal, Soups, Salads, and Sandwiches* cookbook (William Morrow)

PHOTOGRAPH BY CHRISTOPHER GLASIER

Q: What is your favorite comfort food?
A: For a snack I would have to say a jam sandwich! Of course the bread must be country style home baked loaf with a dark crust. The butter would need to be fresh and high quality and the jam homemade and very fruity but not too sweet.
   My favorite comfort hot dish would be my grandmother's braised oxtail with mash potatoes and mushy peas. Her secret being a sprinkle of sugar and dried mint leaves over the peas—fantastic! Served with a Yorkshire pudding!

Q: If you could eat anywhere in the world, where would it be?
A: In the middle east—Iran, Syria, Lebanon. I would love to explore the regional cooking in these areas. Failing that, a plateau de fruits de mers in the south of France with a bottle of chilled rose would suffice!

Q: What food could you live without and why?
A: Tripe. I have eaten it in several ways—blanched and cut into slivers in a salad in Florence, Italy, (this was the most palatable). I have eaten it stewed in duck fat in Lyon, France, (this was far too fatty and strong) and I have eaten it braised with tomatoes in Northern Spain, (texture and flavor both overbearing). I absolutely adore offal especially liver, brains, tongue, cheek, pig's ears/tails etc. but have never taken to tripe.

BLUEBERRY ORANGE SCONES

BY KAREN TRILEVSKY • YIELD: 12 SCONES (APPROXIMATELY)

3	CUPS ALL-PURPOSE FLOUR
½	CUP ROLLED OATS
⅔	CUP SUGAR
1	TEASPOON SALT
½	TEASPOON GROUND CINNAMON
2 ½	TEASPOONS BAKING POWDER
½	TEASPOON BAKING SODA
1½	STICKS UNSALTED BUTTER (6 OUNCES), CHOPPED
1	CUP BUTTERMILK
1	LARGE ORANGE, FINELY ZESTED
1½	CUPS BLUEBERRIES, FRESH OR FROZEN
	EXTRA SUGAR FOR TOP OF SCONES

Preheat the oven to 375 °. Grease cookie sheet with pan spray, and set aside.

In a large bowl, mix together flour, oats, sugar, salt, cinnamon, baking powder and baking soda. Add butter, mix with hands until butter is size of oat pieces. Add buttermilk and orange zest. Mix until just combined. Gently stir in blueberries.

Scoop batter into rounds on cookie sheet, about ⅓ cup in size. Sprinkle tops with granulated sugar. Bake for 18 to 20 minutes, or until lightly brown at edges.

Cool 5 minutes, use metal spatula to remove from pan.

She was hungry.

Consumed with a desire to find a better way, FullBloom Baking Co. founder Karen Trilevsky wanted to build a company that cared about its people and its planet. With a commitment to providing real living wages and offering educational opportunities for all families, she built a socially conscious and unswervingly ethical business. And she continues to do it in a way that's ecologically responsible and agriculturally sustainable. Oh, and they make a damn good scone while they're at it.

Founded in 1989, FullBloom has grown from one who cared to over 200.

FULLBLOOM BAKING CO.

Q: What put you on the culinary career path?
A: Being a hungry runaway. Restaurant kitchens have always been a great place for 'misfits'—you could assume a new name, identity, age, whatever. Just be willing to work hard—you'll get paid and fed!

Q: If not for food, where would you be now?
A: Medicine—neurosurgery or 'alternative' therapies.

Q: If you could eat anywhere in the world, where would it be?
A: Thailand or Vietnam.

NOODLE KUGEL WITH PEARS, WALNUTS, AND APRICOTS

BY FAYE LEVY • SERVES 8

4	TABLESPOONS PLUS 2 TABLE-SPOONS PLUS 1 TEASPOON BUTTER OR MARGARINE
14	OUNCES MEDIUM EGG NOODLES
1	PINCH SALT
1¼	POUNDS PEARS, RIPE BUT FIRM
4	TABLESPOONS PLUS 2 TABLE-SPOONS SUGAR
¾	TEASPOON PLUS ¾ TEASPOON GROUND CINNAMON
1	TEASPOON GRATED LEMON ZEST
1	TEASPOON GRATED ORANGE ZEST
½	CUP DICED DRIED APRICOTS
½	CUP WALNUTS, CHOPPED
4	LARGE EGGS, SEPARATED

Preheat the oven to 350°.

Grease a 13 x 9 x 2-inch baking dish with a teaspoon or less of butter or margarine.

Cook noodles in a large pot of boiling salted water uncovered over high heat for 5 minutes, or until barely tender. Drain, rinse with cold water, and drain again. Transfer to a large bowl.

Meanwhile, peel, core, halve and slice pears about ¼ inch thick. Heat 2 tablespoons butter or margarine in a large skillet. Add half of pears and sauté over medium heat for 3 minutes, turning once. Remove with a slotted spoon. Add remaining pears to skillet and sauté. When done, return all pears to skillet. Sprinkle with 2 tablespoons sugar and ¾ teaspoon cinnamon and sauté for 1 minute more, turning pears gently to coat. Transfer to a bowl.

Add 4 tablespoons butter or margarine to skillet and melt it over low heat. Add 3 tablespoons of the melted butter to the noodles and reserve 1 tablespoon. Add lemon and orange zest to the noodles and mix well. Stir in apricots and walnuts.

In a large bowl, whip egg whites with electric mixer to form soft peaks. Beat in remaining 4 tablespoons sugar and whip at high speed for 20 seconds, or until whites are stiff but not dry.

Stir egg yolks into noodles. Stir in one-fourth of the whipped whites. Fold in remaining whites.

Add half of noodle mixture to greased baking dish. Top with an even layer of pears. Top the pears with the remaining noodle mixture and spread gently to cover completely. Sprinkle with ¾ teaspoon of cinnamon, then the remaining 1 tablespoon melted butter.

Cover kugel with aluminum foil and bake for 30 minutes. Uncover and bake for an additional 15 to 20 minutes, or until set. Serve hot or warm.

Serving suggestion: Perfect with sour cream or raspberry sauce

Note: Advanced preparation: Keep the baked kugel covered in its baking dish in the refrigerator. Reheat covered at about 300°.

BREAD WITH CHOCOLATE
PAN CON CHOCOLATE

BY KAT FUKUSHIMA · SERVES 4

This is a quick and easy way of making classic Spanish bread with chocolate. You will need either a grill or a toaster oven.

4	SLICES QUALITY BREAD, EACH ¾ INCH THICK
	EXTRA VIRGIN OLIVE OIL, PREFERABLY YOUNG, FRESH, SPANISH
2	OUNCES BITTERSWEET CHOCOLATE
	MALDON SEA SALT, COARSE
1	ORANGE

Lightly brush both sides of the bread with the olive oil. Brown on the grill or place in a toaster oven until golden brown.

With a coarse grater, quickly grate the chocolate over the hot bread.

Drizzle the bread with more olive oil and sprinkle on some Maldon salt.

Spank the orange with your zester to awaken the oils and aromas. Zest the orange over the bread.

Serve immediately. If you want to have really nice hot melting chocolate, flash the chocolate bread in the toaster oven.

ABOUT KAT FUKUSHIMA
www.cafeatlantico.com
(see Appetizers, page 58)

BREAD WITH CHOCOLATE

PERSIAN PISTACHIO SOUP
SUP-E PESTEH

BY NAJMIEH BATMANGLIJ · SERVES 6

The word "pistachio" comes from the Persian word pesteh and one ancient nickname for the Persian people was "pistachio-eaters." According to a Greek chronicler, when King Astyages of the Medes in the fifth century B.C. gazed from his throne over his army, which had been defeated by Cyrus the Great, he exclaimed, "Woe, how brave are these pistachio-eating Persians!"

GARNISH

1	TABLESPOON VEGETABLE OIL
½	CUP SHELLED PISTACHIOS
½	CUP DRIED BARBERRIES
1	TEASPOON SUGAR

SOUP

2	TABLESPOONS VEGETABLE OIL
1	SMALL ONION, FINELY CHOPPED
2	LEEKS (WHITE AND GREEN PARTS), FINELY CHOPPED
1	1-INCH PIECE OF FRESH GINGER, GRATED
2	CLOVES GARLIC, PEELED AND GRATED
1	THAI BIRD CHILI, CHOPPED OR ¼ TEASPOON CHILI FLAKES
2	TABLESPOONS GROUND CUMIN
1	TEASPOON GROUND CORIANDER
1	TEASPOON SALT
1	TEASPOON FRESHLY GROUND BLACK PEPPER
¼	TEASPOON GROUND TURMERIC
1	CUP RICE FLOUR
1	CUP UNSALTED PISTACHIOS, GROUND

Garnish: To prepare the garnish, heat 1 tablespoon oil in a heavy-based, medium-sized pot over medium heat. Add ½ cup shelled whole pistachios, ½ cup cleaned barberries* and 1 teaspoon sugar. Stir-fry for 20 seconds (barberries can burn easily; be careful). Use a slotted spoon to transfer the mixture from the pot to a small bowl. Set aside.

In the same pot, heat 2 tablespoons oil over medium heat until very hot. Add the onion, leeks, ginger, garlic, chili, cumin, coriander, salt, pepper and turmeric. Stir-fry for 1 minute. Reduce heat to low, cover and allow to stew gently for 5 to 10 minutes.

Add the rice flour and stir-fry for 2 minutes. Add the ground pistachios and 2 cups broth or water. Whisk constantly, until smooth and bring to a boil.

Add the rest of the broth or water and bring back to a boil. Reduce heat, cover and simmer over low heat for 45 minutes, stirring occasionally.

Use a hand-held mixer or immersion blender to purée the ingredients in the soup. Check for consistency and add more broth if the soup is too thick for your taste.

Just before serving, add the orange and lime juice mixture and adjust seasoning to taste. Cover and keep warm until ready to serve.

To serve, place 1 tablespoon of garnish in each of six warm soup bowls and pour in 1 ladle full of soup. Serve with crisp hot bread.

***Note:** Dried barberries must be thoroughly cleaned before cooking. Stem the berries, place in a fine-mesh colander, partly immerse in cold water and let it soak for 10 minutes. Remove from the water, run fresh cold water over the berries and drain.

5   CUPS PLUS 2 CUPS CHICKEN
        BROOTH OR WATER
¾   CUP FRESH ORANGE JUICE MIXED
        WITH ¼ CUP FRESH LIME JUICE

Wine note: An amazing set of flavors and textures are found in this pale, creamy soup. The pistachio spice really comes through, combining with the barberry garnish to balance the rich soup. White wine is best here; a Pinot Gris or a Viognier can stand up to this soup without overwhelming.

PERSIAN PISTACHIO SOUP

ABOUT NAJMIEH BATMANGLIJ

Introducing people to the pleasures of Persian cuisine has been a lifelong mission for Najmieh Batmanglij. Her book *New Food of Life: Ancient Persian and Modern Iranian Cooking and Ceremonies* was called "the definitive book of Persian cooking" by the *Los Angeles Times,* and her *Silk Road Cooking: A Vegetarian Journey* was selected as one of the Vegetarian Cookbooks of 2004 by the *New York Times.* Her latest book, *From Persia to NapA: Wine at the Persian Table* was published in September 2006.

Najmieh Batmanglij has spent the past 26 years traveling, teaching cooking, and adapting authentic Persian recipes to tastes and techniques in the West. She is a member of Les Dames d'Escoffier and has taught and lectured throughout the United States. She currently lives in Washington, DC, where she is teaching master classes in Persian cooking and is working on a new book for children to cook with the family.

ACHIEVEMENTS

* 2002, 2004 *Silk Road Cooking: A Vegetarian Journey* cookbook (Mage)
* 1999-2007 *A Taste of PersiA: An Introduction to Persian Cooking* cookbook (IB Tauris)
* 1994 *Persian Cooking for a Healthy Kitchen* cookbook (Mage)
* 1992–2006 *New Food of Life: Ancient Persian and Modern Iranian Cooking and Ceremonies* cookbook (Mage)
* 1984 *Ma Cuisine d'Iran* cookbook (Paris)

Q: What is your favorite comfort food?
A: A humble meal in Iran known as Nun-o panir-o sabzi khordan, flat crispy bread, goat cheese, fresh herbs (basil, cilantro, mint, tarragon, scallion), crispy baby cucumbers, and walnuts.

Q: If you could eat anywhere in the world, where would it be?
A: In Iran, by the Caspian coast.

Q: If you met Augusta Escoffier, what would you ask?
A: Quelle pays a inspire le plus votre cuisine?

SPICY CORN CHOWDER

BY JEFFREY SPEAR • SERVES 4

2	TABLESPOON OLIVE OIL
2	TABLESPOON BUTTER
1	LARGE ONION, COARSELY GRATED
1	TABLESPOON ALL-PURPOSE FLOUR
4	CUPS CHICKEN OR VEGETABLE STOCK
2	TO 3 LARGE RED POTATOES, PEELED, CUT INTO ½-INCH DICE
4	CUPS CORN (FRESH OR FROZEN)
1½	CUPS WHOLE MILK
	SALT AND PEPPER TO TASTE
	TABASCO TO TASTE
2	TABLESPOONS FINELY CHOPPED CHIVES

In a large pot, heat oil and melt butter. Add onion and sauté until soft, not brown. Add flour and stir for 1-2 minutes until smooth. Add stock gradually, stirring constantly to incorporate the flour. Add potatoes and corn. Bring to a boil, reduce heat and simmer for 30 minutes. Remove from heat.

Transfer half of the soup to a separate bowl. Ladle this soup, a little at a time, into a high-speed blender. Purée until creamy smooth. You can return the soup purée from the blender back into the pot as you go. When complete, add milk, salt, pepper and Tabasco to taste. I like mine a little spicy and tend to be heavy handed with the Tabasco. Return to heat, bring to desired temperature and serve. Garnish with chives.

Note: You can also use an immersion blender right in the pot—taking care not to purée all of the solids. The soup won't be quite as smooth and creamy but much faster to make. Less dishes to wash as well.

Q: What is your favorite comfort food?

A: My favorite comfort food is pasta. When I get home after a long night in the restaurant, I sometimes make myself a bowl of spaghetti.

Q: What put you on the culinary career path?

A: It was my passion for food and encouragement from mentors that got me started. Twenty five years ago I just wanted to cook! I had no idea I would land where I am today—chef/restaurant owner and cookbook author.

Q: If not for food, where would you be now?

A: I have no idea....

Q: If you could eat anywhere in the world, where would it be?

A: Rome.

WEST INDIAN PUMPKIN SOUP

BY CINDY HUTSON • SERVES 8

4	TABLESPOONS BUTTER
1	CUP SLICED ONION
2	CLOVES GARLIC, CRUSHED AND CHOPPED
1	CUP SLICED CELERY
1	CUP SLICED CARROTS
2	TABLESPOONS FINELY GRATED FRESH GINGER
1	SMOKED HAM HOCK
¼	CUP FRESH THYME LEAVES
6	ALLSPICES BERRIES
3	CUPS DICED PUMPKIN
2	QUARTS CHICKEN STOCK
2	TABLESPOONS KOSHER SALT
1	TABLESPOON BLACK PEPPER
	GARNISH WITH NUTMEG CREMA (SEE PAGE 262)

Sauté onions and garlic in the butter in a large stockpot over medium heat.

After the onion-garlic mixture begins to soften, add the celery, carrots and ginger. Continue to sauté on medium heat for about 3-5 minutes. Add the ham hock, thyme and allspice and sauté for 4 minutes.

Add the pumpkin and chicken stock. Bring to boil and then reduce to a simmer until the vegetables are tender.

Since chicken stocks can vary in salt content, taste the soup before adding the 2 tablespoons of kosher salt. You may need less or a bit more. Adjust to taste. Add the fresh ground pepper. Remove the ham hock.

Let the soup cool for 30 minutes. Using a blender, purée the soup in small batches. When blending hot sauces or soups in a blender, it is necessary to only fill the blender ½ way, remove center cap and cover with a kitchen towel. Otherwise the heat causes the top to explode off and you will get burned.

When ready to serve, garnish with the Nutmeg Crema (page 262).

ABOUT CINDY HUTSON

www.cindyhutsoncuisine.com

Self-taught, Chef Cindy Hutson has been showered with praise since opening her first restaurant, Norma's on the Beach, in 1994. With an emphasis on Jamaican flavors and fresh tropical ingredients, the eatery was touted the Best Caribbean Restaurant in South Florida by publications such as *USA Today, The New York Times* and *London Times* and was recognized with the coveted Five Star Diamond.

Her 1999 venture Ortanique featured Hutson's new concept, "Cuisine of the Sun," which combined South American, Asian, Caribbean, and American Fusion influences to create imaginative dishes with seasonal fruits, fish, meats and exotic seasonings.

Ortanique received the *Wine Spectator* Award of Excellence. Five Star Diamond Award, Mobil Four Stars and Best New Restaurant from *Esquire Magazine,* to name a few.

ACHIEVEMENTS

- 2002, 2003, 2004, 2005 "Award of Excellence," *Wine Spectator*
- 2004 "America's Top Tables," *Gourmet*
- 1999, 2003 and 2004 "Exceptional" (Top Rating), *Miami Herald*
- 1999 "Best New Restaurant in America," *Esquire Magazine*

ORTANIQUE

Q: Was your mother a good cook? What is your mother's best dish and can you duplicate it?

A: My mother was not a very good cook at all. She was, and still is a fabulous mother who enjoys her family and their friends so much that she would painstakingly fix huge dinner feasts and invite everyone to join us for dinner and lots of laughs. We had so many wonderful gatherings around our dinner table. It has made me realize that old adage "Home is where the heart is." Whether I am in my own home now with my children and family or at my restaurant, the table is always set with love.

GAZPACHO OLE

BY DARA BUNJON • SERVES 8

Soup

46	OUNCES TOMATO JUICE
1	MEDIUM GREEN PEPPER, SEEDED, ROUGHLY CHOPPED, HALVED
1	CUCUMBER, ENDS REMOVED, ROUGHLY CHOPPED, HALVED
1	MEDIUM RED ONION, PEELED, ROUGHLY CHOPPED, HALVED
2	LARGE TOMATOES, ROUGHLY CHOPPED, HALVED
5	RADISHES, TRIMMED AND ROUGHLY CHOPPED, HALVED
1	CLOVE PLUS 1 CLOVE GARLIC
½	CUP PLUS ½ CUP EXTRA VIRGIN OLIVE OIL
1	LIME, ZESTED FINE AND JUICED, RESERVED SEPARATELY
⅓	CUP SHERRY VINEGAR, DIVIDED IN HALF
	SALT TO TASTE

Tortilla Croutons

1	TEASPOON GROUND CUMIN
¼	TEASPOON FINE SEA SALT OR KOSHER SALT
¼	CUP CANOLA OIL
3	8-INCH CORN TORTILLAS, CUT INTO ¼-INCH BY 3-INCH STRIPS

To prepare the soup: In a very large bowl pour the tomato juice. You will be adding to it later

The soup is made in two batches in a blender. In the first batch, add half the green pepper, cucumber, red onion, tomatoes, radishes, garlic, extra virgin olive oil, lime juice and sherry vinegar to your blender. Start to blend on slow and then increase to high. When processed, pour the contents into the bowl with the tomato juice. Repeat the same process for the 2nd batch. Stir well, then chill.

To prepare the tortilla croutons: Combine the reserved lime zest, ground cumin and sea salt.

Heat the oil in a 12 inch fry pan until near smoking. Add the tortilla strips and fry till lightly golden and crunchy.

Drain the tortilla strips on paper towel. Immediately dust with the lime, cumin and salt mixture. Croutons can be made up to 24 hours ahead and stored in an airtight container. There will be plenty so treat the cook and enjoy a few.

Serve the soup in chilled bowls and top with the Tortilla Croutons.

Note: Put a personal touch on this soup with some poached shelled shrimp, scallops, or crabmeat.

ABOUT DARA BUNJON

http:www.dara-does-it.com

http:www.diningdish.blogspot.com

Dara Bunjon's passion for food—its origins, preparation and consumption—has her hands in assorted aspects of the food industry. Bunjon started her culinary endeavors as president of the Epicurean Club of Maryland that organized cooking classes in restaurant kitchens. She then moved on to supporting charitable activities to end hunger. A stint as Marketing and Public Relations Director for Vanns Spices also called upon her culinary knowledge for product development and sales. Most recently, she launched a consulting business: Dara Does It—Creative Solutions for the Food Industry.

Once a regular cooking personality on WBAL-TV's early news in Baltimore, you now find Dara behind the scenes as a food stylist for chefs and cookbook authors, a public relations and marketing agent for restaurants and food related businesses and planning special culinary events.

Dara is a board member for the Maryland Hospitality Education Foundation and the American Institute of Wine and Food/Baltimore, MD, as well as a member of the national public relations committee for Women Chefs and Restaurateurs. She is a contributing writer for *Foodservice Monthly* and has written for *Style Magazine, Mid-Atlantic Restaurant Digest, Urbanite* and assorted websites. Known as Dining Dish to many in the Baltimore/DC area, Dara writes a free 'foodie' e-newsletter under the same name and maintains a food-related blog.

Bunjon was key in reaching out to the culinary experts who have donated recipes to this book, coordinated recipe testing and provided invaluable insights towards the creation of this cookbook.

Q: What put you on the culinary career path?
A: Hunger.

Q: If you were condemned to die, what would be your last meal?
A: Steamed lobsters—note the plural (I take a long time to eat shellfish), perfectly seared foie gras with a lobster side and a dozen steamed crabs. That would take me about 3 hours. The finale, a moist yellow cake with a fudge icing.

Q: If not for food, where would you be now?
A: Working the runways in Milan.

ABOUT ANA SORTUN

www.oleanarestaurant.com www.sienafarms.com

In her memoir, *Eating My Words*, food writer Mimi Sheraton
included Ana Sortun as one of the country's "best creative fusion
practitioners," describing the chef's food as "inspired and inspiring." With a degree from La Varenne Ecole de Cuisine in Paris,
the Seattle-born Sortun opened Moncef Medeb's Aigo Bistro in
Concord, Massachusetts, in the early 1990s. Stints at 8 Holyoke
and Casablanca in Harvard Square, Cambridge soon followed.
When Sortun opened Oleana in 2001, she quickly drew raves for
her creative combination of farm-fresh ingredients and eastern
Mediterranean spice blends. Sortun's food, explained Catherine
Reynolds in the *New York Times*, "is at once rustic-traditional and
deeply inventive." After a visit to Boston, Tom Sietsema of the
Washington Post wrote of Oleana, "Should you have time for only
one place to eat, make it this space." The judges of the Beard
Foundation awards certainly agreed, as they awarded Sortun The
Best Chef: Northeast honor in 2005.

Chef Sortun's cookbook, *SPICE; flavors of the Eastern
Mediterranean*, published in 2006, is already a best seller according
to the *Boston Globe* and the *LA Times*. "This is not fusion food, nor
has Sortun forced any technique or tradition. Instead she has
allowed the flavors of the regional food, and her tangible love of it,
to determine her cooking—and her cookbook," says Amy
Scattergood of the *LA Times*. 2006 also brought the addition of
Siena farms, owned and farmed by Chef Sortun's husband, Chris
Kurth. The farm, named after their baby daughter Siena, provides
the restaurant all of its fresh organic produce.

ELEGANT OYSTER SOUP

ELEGANT OYSTER SOUP

BY JOANNA PRUESS • SERVES 4

One fine October day some years ago, an acquaintance returned from the oyster festival in St. Mary's, Maryland, where she had consumed more than her quotient of the "best fried, poached, scalloped and raw oysters I ever tasted." Dropping a pint jar of shucked creatures on my counter, she threw down the gauntlet and challenged my creativity. This sublime soup of gently poached plump, succulent oysters perfumed with parsley pesto was the result. It is just hearty enough for a light supper or, in cups, as a start to an elegant dinner.

1	LARGE CARROT, SCRAPED
1	LARGE RIB CELERY, TRIMMED
1	LARGE ONION, PEELED
1	LARGE CLOVE GARLIC
2	TEASPOONS UNSALTED BUTTER OR OLIVE OIL
1	TEASPOON VEGETABLE OIL
½	CUP DRY VERMOUTH
2	CUPS HALF-&-HALF
1½	CUPS CLAM BROTH
1	PINT SHUCKED OYSTERS AND THEIR LIQUOR
	SALT AND WHITE PEPPER
	LEMON PARSLEY PESTO (SEE PAGE 261)

Finely chop the carrot, celery, onion, and remaining garlic clove either by hand or in a food processor. If using a processor, pulse the vegetables so you don't over chop them. Heat the butter and oil in a large heavy pot over medium-high heat. When hot, stir in the vegetables and sauté until lightly browned, 3 to 4 minutes, stirring occasionally. Cover, adjust the heat to low, and sweat the vegetables until soft, 5 minutes more.

Pour in the vermouth, stirring up any browned cooking bits, and bring the liquid to a boil for 1 minute. Stir in the half-and-half and simmer for 5 minute. Transfer the mixture to the jar of an electric blender and purée until smooth.

Return the purée to the pot, stir in the clam broth, and bring the liquid to a simmer. Add the oysters and their liquor, and poach until barely done, 5 to 7 minutes. Season to taste with salt and white pepper. Ladle the soup into cups or bowls and serve with about 1 tablespoon of pesto in the center of each bowl (or ½ tablespoon for a cup).

Joanna Pruess' most recent cookbooks are *Seduced by Bacon: Recipes and Lore about America's Favorite Indulgence* (The Lyons Press, 2006) and *FiammA: The Essence of Contemporary Italian Cooking with Michael White* (John Wiley & Sons, 2006). An award-winning author, she has also written extensively on food for publications including *The*

New York Times Sunday Magazine, The Washington Post, Food Arts, Saveur, Food & Wine and the Associated Press syndicate. She is well-known in the specialty food business as a consultant, as well as a regular contributor to NASFT's *Specialty Foods Magazine* and as a speaker at many shows. She has developed recipes for clients including Bella Cucina Artful Food, Bigelow Tea, Stonewall Kitchen, Sarabeth's Kitchen, More Than Gourmet, Dufour Pastry Kitchens, and Vanns Spices.

Joanna Pruess created and was the first director of the Cookingstudio, a cooking school within Kings Super Market in New Jersey, where she had more than 15,000 students in five years. Among the many classes she taught were specially created courses for those with visual or hearing impairments, as well as those with learning disabilities. Pruess was the subject of a profile in *Bon Appetit* and *People,* as well as several other publications. She appeared regularly of WYNY's "Good Day, New York" and was honored by NYU's School of Food Service as Woman of the Year in Food Service, Merchandising and Promotion.

She is married to WCBS and *Crain's New York Business* restaurant critic Bob Lape and they reside in the Bronx, New York.

Q: If not for food, where would you be now?

A: I would probably have continued as a fashion designer and stylist. However, the economy was flat and no one was buying the couture clothes and accessories that I made. Fortunately I was able to fall back on my love of food. From being a food savvy fashionista, I became a fashionable "foodie" and started the Cookingstudio in Kings Super Markets.

Q: What put you on the culinary career path?

A: Ironically, it was seeing Audrey Hepburn in *Sabrina* that started me on my culinary path. In that movie, she went to Le Cordon Bleu in Paris, where she learned to crack an egg with one hand. I wanted to be like her and thus set off to Paris and that school.

Salads

BELGIAN ENDIVE AND ORANGE SALAD

BELGIAN ENDIVE AND ORANGE SALAD

BY SUSANNA FOO • FROM HER BOOK *SUSANNA FOO FRESH INSPIRATION*
SERVES 4

2	BELGIAN ENDIVES
3	NAVEL ORANGES
6	TABLESPOONS SOUR CREAM
¼	CUP PLUS 2 TABLESPOONS CITRUS VINAIGRETTE (SEE PAGE 256)
1	TEASPOON SUGAR
2	CUPS BABY ARUGULA

Slice the Belgian endive in half, lengthwise. Remove the hard inner core and discard. Cut the endive, crosswise, into half-circle pieces, about ¼ inch thick. Place into a bowl and cover with ice cold water. Let soak for 10 minutes. Drain the endive well, making sure the pieces are very dry and refrigerate until needed.

Remove the skin from the oranges and cut into segments. Cut the segments from one orange into ½-inch pieces. Reserve the other two as whole segments.

Using a medium sized bowl, mix together the sour cream, citrus vinaigrette, and the sugar. Mix in the endive, arugula and the diced orange segments.

Mound the salad into the center of four chilled salad plates. Decorate by placing the orange segments around the endive, a drizzle of the Citrus Vinaigrette and serve.

Note: From December to late spring, when blood oranges are in season, make this salad with them instead of navel oranges. It will look even more striking. The components for the salad can be readied in advance and refrigerated - but mix in the orange pieces right before serving so the dressing will not become watery.

ABOUT SUSANNA FOO

www.susannafoo.com

Born China and raised in Taiwan, Foo became well acquainted with the regions spices, grains, and produce. She has fond memories of learning to wrap dumplings with her grandmother, and owes her mother-in-law and cousin for teaching her about Hunan style cuisine and Chinese Northern-style pasta making.

Foo originally came to America to pursue a degree in library science. Fate had its way. In 1979, she and her husband, E-Hsin, moved to Philadelphia to join his family's business where they opened Hu-Nan.

While cooking at Hu-Nan, Foo met Jacob Rosenthal (founder, Culinary Institute of America). Rosenthal encouraged her to study at the CIA where she quickly mastered French techniques. In 1987, she opened Susanna Foo Chinese Cuisine.

In 2003, Foo opened Suilan by Susanna Foo in Atlantic City. Suilan offers her French-influenced dishes and a menu in Chinese.

In 2006, Susanna Foo Gourmet Kitchen opened in Radnor, Pennsylvania. The farm-fresh, family-friendly cuisine is inspired by the simple, flavorful dishes reminiscent of the Chinese dumpling houses Susanna loved to eat in when she was growing up in China.

Chef Foo is regarded as one of the country's top Chinese chefs. She has authored two critically acclaimed cookbooks and honored with dozens of culinary awards. She was named to the first group of *Food & Wine Magazine's* "10 Best New Chefs," the coveted Robert Mondavi Culinary Award of Excellence in 1999, and two James Beard awards.

Every year, she returns to her homeland, spending time in Inner Mongolia, Shanghai, and Taiwan with the friends and family who were integral in her culinary education.

ACHIEVEMENTS

- 2005 *Susanna Foo Fresh Inspiration* cookbook
- 2003 Suilan named *Esquire's* "Best New Restaurant of the Year"
- 1995 *Susanna Foo Chinese Cuisine* cookbook

Q: What is your favorite comfort food?
A: My favorite comfort food is Braised Stew (either with Beef or Pork).

Q: If not for food, where would you be now?
A: A gardener.

Q: What is your favorite family recipe?
A: Pork dumplings.

Q: What food could you live without?
A: Cottage cheese.

CHARLOTTE OF ASPARAGUS AND CRAB

BY NATHALIE DUPREE • SERVES 4

1 POUND GREEN ASPARAGUS
    SALT TO TASTE
    OLIVE OIL
1 CUP HOMEMADE OR PREPARED
    MAYONNAISE
2 TABLESPOONS KETCHUP
1 POUND CRABMEAT, PICKED OVER
    FOR SHELLS
1 ORANGE, JUICED AND ZESTED
½ CUP OLIVE OIL (½ TO 1 CUP)
1 SHALLOT, FINELY CHOPPED
3 RIPE SMALL OR MEDIUM
    TOMATOES, PEELED, SLICED,
    AND CHOPPED

OPTIONAL GARNISHES:
    FENNEL OR DILL FROND
    LEMON, CUT UP OR DECORATED

If the asparagus is large, or the skin is tough, peel with a knife or a vegetable peeler, holding the asparagus flat on the board and turning the asparagus as the peeler works down from the top. After you have gone around the entire asparagus, cut off the bottom where the peeler has stopped on the tough stem. Tie the asparagus together, facing the same way, and drop into a pot of rapidly boiling water, salted to taste. Cook 3 to 4 minutes. A knife inserted easily just under the last "flower" at the top of the asparagus indicates it is cooked. Remove, drain and run under cold water to stop the cooking. Cut off the small, pointed tips of the asparagus and set aside. If the tips are large, cut them in half lengthwise. If the stems are large, cut them in half lengthwise.

Oil a small soufflé mold, a charlotte mold or even a straight-sided muffin cup approximately 6 to 8 ounces. Insert plastic wrap if you wish to facilitate removal later.

Line the mold with asparagus stems cut evenly to the top of the mold. Thin the mayonnaise, if thick, with a tablespoon or so of hot water. Add enough ketchup to color the mayonnaise. Taste. Stir in the crabmeat. Chop up and add any extra asparagus stems. (May be made a day in advance.) Pack tightly into the molds and chill thoroughly.

Mix the juice and zest of the orange and whisk in the olive oil. Add the shallot and tomatoes. When you are ready to serve, remove the plastic wrap and its contents carefully by putting an oiled plate on top and turning the plate to release the filling onto the plate. Shape, if necessary, with your hands. Garnish with the vinaigrette, fennel or dill and lemon. Alternatively, just pass the vinaigrette.

CAESAR SALAD
WITH CRISPY OYSTERS

CAESAR SALAD WITH CRISPY OYSTERS

BY CHRISTINE KEFF • SERVES 6

18	SHUCKED OYSTERS
1	CUP CORNMEAL
	CANOLA OIL FOR FRYING
2	HEADS ROMAINE HEARTS, SEPARATED INTO LEAVES
	CAESAR DRESSING (SEE PAGE 254)
1	2-INCH PIECE PARMESAN CHEESE

Bread the oysters in the cornmeal. Heat 2 inches of oil to 340° in a shallow pan. Drop the oysters into the oil in batches of 4 or 5. When crispy and golden brown, remove from oil and drain on toweling.

Toss the romaine leaves in enough Caesar dressing to coat. Put the oysters on top and shave long slices of Parmesan cheese on the salad.

Wine note: Goes well with a Semillon/Sauvignon blend.

Q: Was your mother a good cook? What is your mother's best dish and can you duplicate it?

A: My Mom was a good cook, though actually it was my Dad who taught her. Of course, once she had it down, he disappeared from the kitchen. She cooked a lot of Southern food even though we were in California, because Dad was from New Orleans and that's what he knew. She made a great red beans and rice; I've never had any better. Pretty good for a Midwest gal. I make it often; the secret is a meaty hamhock.

Q: If you could eat anywhere in the world, where would it be?

A: I've been lucky enough to eat all over the world—France, Italy, Spain, Greece, Japan, Vietnam, Thailand, Indonesia, Mexico—but I've yet to get to India. That's where I'd like to eat.

WATERMELON AND GREEN TOMATO SALAD

BY SCOTT PEACOCK · SERVES 4

FOR THE DRESSING:

3	TABLESPOONS RED WINE VINEGAR
2	TABLESPOONS FRESHLY SQUEEZED ORANGE JUICE
2	TEASPOONS HONEY
2	TEASPOONS GRATED, SEEDED HOT GREEN CHILE (JALAPEÑO OR SERRANO)
1	SMALL GARLIC CLOVE, CUT IN HALF
½	TEASPOON SALT
½	TEASPOON FRESHLY GROUND BLACK PEPPER
½	CUP EXTRA VIRGIN OLIVE OIL

FOR THE FRUIT SALAD:

6	CUPS SEEDLESS WATERMELON, CUT INTO ¾-INCH PIECES
1	MEDIUM GREEN TOMATO (OR 2 HUSKED TOMATILLOS), CORED, HALVED AND THINLY SLICED
½	CUP VIDALIA ONION SLICED INTO THIN HALF MOONS, SOAKED IN ICE WATER FOR 20 MINUTES
¼	CUP FRESH MINT LEAVES
4	CUPS ARUGULA LEAVES

To make the dressing: Put the red wine vinegar, orange juice, honey, chile, garlic clove, salt, and pepper in a non-reactive mixing bowl. Stir to blend and let sit for 10 minutes.

Remove the garlic clove and whisk in the oil, taste carefully and adjust seasoning as desired.

To assemble the salad: In a large bowl combine the watermelon, green tomato, drained and blotted dry Vidalia onion and fresh mint leaves. Add arugula and the dressing. Toss gently to mix. Taste for seasoning once again. Serve immediately.

ABOUT SCOTT PEACOCK
www.watershedrestaurant.com

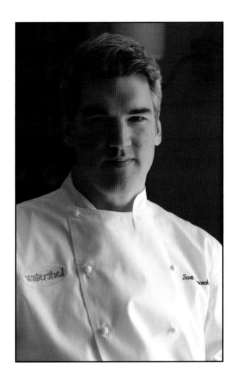

Watershed's executive chef, Scott Peacock, is the former chef to two Georgia governors and was founding chef of Atlanta's Horseradish Grill. He is a Southern food expert whose vision of Southern cuisine emphasizes fresh, seasonal, regionally grown ingredients of the highest integrity, prepared with the barest of embellishments.

Chef Peacock's ideas and recipes have been featured in many national and local publications including: *Newsweek, The New York Times, The Wine Spectator, Bon Appetit, Food and Wine, USA Today, Atlanta Magazine, Gourmet, Cooking Light, Southern Living* and many more.

Presently, in addition to creating dishes at Watershed, Peacock has written a cookbook, *The Gift of Southern Cooking: Recipes and Revelations from two Southern Chefs,* with his friend and mentor, the late Edna Lewis, considered America's foremost authority on traditional southern cooking.

Chef Peacock has been twice nominated by the James Beard Foundation for Best Chef in the Southeast.

Q: If not for food, where would you be now?
A: If not for food, I would probably be miserably sweeping floors in an Alabama auto parts store.

Q: Was your mother a good cook? What is your mother's best dish and can you duplicate it?
A: Yes my mother is a good cook, and yes, I do a pretty good version of her cobbler that makes me happy. Her cobbler is my favorite family recipe.

Q: What is your favorite comfort food?
A: My favorite comfort food is ice cream. Big, endless bowls of ice cream.

COLD-POACHED SALMON WITH HEARTS OF PALM AND TAMARIND

BY CHARLIE TROTTER • FROM HIS BOOK *ONE&ONLY PALMILLA SPA CUISINE BY CHARLIE TROTTER*
SERVES 4

Cold poaching the fish ensures that it will be moist and delicate. It also transforms the court bouillon you use for the poaching liquid into a nicely flavored fish stock that can be used for another recipe. You may opt to cook the salmon by another method, such as slow roasting or sous vide.

FOR THE SALMON

4   4 OUNCE SALMON FILETS SKIN REMOVED

     KOSHER SALT AND FRESHLY GROUND BLACK PEPPER

3   CUPS COURT BOUILLON*, SIMMERING

2   TEASPOONS FINELY GRATED LEMON ZEST

1   TABLESPOON FINELY CHOPPED FRESH CHIVES

FOR THE SALAD

2   CUPS THINLY SLICED HEARTS OF PALM

1   CUP ORANGE SEGMENTS

4   TABLESPOONS PLUS 2 TABLESPOONS OF TAMARIND JUICE (PASTE THINNED WITH WATER)

2   TEASPOONS FRESHLY SQUEEZED LIME JUICE

1   TABLESPOON OLIVE OIL

     KOSHER SALT AND FRESHLY GROUND BLACK PEPPER

4   CUPS LOOSELY PACKED MÂCHE

To prepare the salmon: Season the salmon with $\frac{1}{8}$ teaspoon each salt and pepper and place in a small baking dish.

Pour the simmering Court Bouillon over the salmon and cover. Allow the salmon to cook slowly in the hot liquid for 5 minutes, then turn the salmon over and allow it to sit in the hot liquid for about 5 minutes longer, or until cooked medium.

Carefully remove the salmon from the liquid, season the salmon lightly with salt and pepper, and sprinkle with the lemon zest and chives. Let cool to room temperature. The Court Bouillon can be reserved for another use or discarded.

To prepare the salad: Combine the hearts of palm, orange segments, 2 tablespoons of the tamarind juice, the lime juice, and the olive oil in a bowl and toss to mix. Season with $\frac{1}{8}$ teaspoon each salt and pepper and toss again. Fold in the mâche just before serving.

To assemble each plate: Drizzle 1 tablespoon of the remaining tamarind juice in a random pattern on each plate. Arrange a bed of the salad in the center of each plate and top with a piece of salmon.

*Note: Court Bouillon is a basic stock used for poaching (see Special Ingredients, page 16).

COLD-POACHED SALMON WITH HEARTS OF PALM AND TAMARIND

ABOUT PENNY GREY

www.greygourmet.com

Penny Grey has a background in film and television, including five years as producer and senior producer with public television in Ontario, Canada. She produced "Day Of The Disabled," a five hour evening special focusing on disability issues which won the Judge George Ferguson Award, Ontario March of Dimes. She produced a half hour show in a series for Seniors which won Honourable Mention at the Columbus International Film and Video Festival.

For many years Grey has been interested in cooking. She has regularly made bread for her family for over 30 years and when her children were young, they would plead for store bought bread as a treat. (In adulthood, they agree that homemade bread has its merits!)

Her interest in cooking and baking led to the discovery of the classic rasp, in her husband's woodworking catalogue: The rasp had a lemon next to it and the copy suggested that it was an excellent lemon zester. Its wonderful performance prompted her to seek out Richard and Jeff Grace at Microplane® and assisted in developing a grater designed especially for the kitchen.

Grey Gourmet Inc. opened up the UK and Canadian markets. Penny is affectionately called Mrs. Microplane® by some of her customers because of her enthusiasm for Microplane® graters and her creative suggestions for using the whole Microplane® range in original ways.

Q: What is your favorite comfort food?
A: My favourite comfort food is macaroni and cheese. The British call this kind of dish nursery food because it's often given to youngsters. You must have homemade macaroni and cheese, definitely not the pre-measured store bought kind!

Q: What food could you live without and why?
A: I can remember as a child my father sometimes eating tripe and onions. At the time I thought it looked very unappealing, but the texture was appalling—like rubber. Maybe it wasn't cooked very well, but I don't think I could bring myself to eat any today even though I understand in some quarters it's considered a good addition to a menu.

MANGO WITH RED ONION

ABOUT JOSE ANDRÉS

www.cafeatlantico.com

José Andrés is an internationally recognized culinary innovator who is widely credited with bringing the small plates concept to the United States.

Since arriving in Washington, DC in 1993 to head the kitchen at Jaleo, Andrés has taken on executive chef responsibilities at neighboring Café Atlantico and Zaytinya and, his most adventurous project to date, the minibar by josé andrés at Café Atlantico.

Bon Appetit magazine named Andrés Chef of the Year in the fall of 2004. In 2003, Andrés won the James Beard Foundation's Best Chef of the Mid-Atlantic Region. Andrés also has been featured in leading food magazines such as *SAVEUR, Gourmet,* and *Food & Wine,* as well as "Fox Sunday Morning News with Chris Wallace," the Food Network, *The New York Times, The Washington Post,* and *USA Today.*

Andrés is the popular host of "Vamos a cocinar" a cooking program aired in Spain on TVE and around the world TVE Internacional. His first cookbook, *Tapas: A Taste of Spain in America,* was a best seller in the US and Spain where it was published as *Los Fogones de Jose Andres.*

When he is not in the kitchen, Andrés serves on the board of DC Central Kitchen, is a contributing editor to *Food Arts,* and is an enthusiastic promoter of the Washington restaurant scene. He lives in Washington with his wife Patricia and their three daughters.

Q: If you were condemned to die, what would be your last meal?

A: Pancakes with maple syrup. My girls and I cook them together and we add our special touch: we use olive oil. Extra crispy.

Q: If not for food, where would you be now?

A: Food has opened so many doors for me and taken me places I never thought I'd go. If not a cook, I'd definitely be doing something creative. Maybe the stage? Maybe a painter?

Main Courses

ABOUT SARA MOULTON

www.saramoulton.com

Sara Moulton is a celebrated master in the male-dominated culinary world with credentials that hold their own. She graduated with high honors from the Culinary Institute of America, worked in restaurants for seven years, instructed at The Institute of Culinary Education (formerly Peter Kump's New York Cooking School) and co-founded the New York Women's Culinary Alliance, an "old girls network" for women in the culinary industry.

Moulton is currently the Executive Chef of *Gourmet* Magazine, host of "Sara's Secrets" on the Food Network and the Food Editor for ABC-TV's "Good Morning America." Moulton is the author of two best-selling cook books; *Sara Moulton Cooks at Home*, published in 2002, and most recently, *Sara's Secret for Weeknight Meals*, published in 2005. Moulton's mission as both author and television host is to counter America's disastrous love affair with fast food by encouraging everyone to cook delicious and healthy food at home and to dine with family and friends.

ACHIEVEMENTS

- "Sara's Secrets" television show on The Food Network (2002-present)
- 2005 *Sara's Secrets for Weeknight Meals* cookbook (Broadway Books)
- 2003 Nominated, James Beard Book Award, "General Cookbook for Everyday," (for *Sara Moulton Cooks at Home*)
- 2002 Inducted, James Beard Award, "Who's Who in American Food & Wine"
- *Sara Moulton Cooks at Home* (2001 Broadway Books)

Q: What put you on the culinary career path?
A: I love to eat, that plus having a family of great cooks.

Q: If you were condemned to die, what would be your last meal?
A: Peking duck, cheese, French fries and really good red wine.

CRANBERRY-TERIYAKI LAMB RACK WITH COUSCOUS SALAD

BY MING TSAI • FROM HIS BOOK *MING'S MASTER RECIPES*
SERVES 4

2	NATURALLY FED LAMB RACKS, FAT CAP REMOVED
1	CUP CRANBERRY-TERIYAKI GLAZE (SEE PAGE 257)
	KOSHER SALT AND FRESHLY GROUND BLACK PEPPER
	GRAPESEED OR CANOLA OIL FOR COOKING
1	LEMON, JUICED AND FINELY ZESTED
1	TABLESPOON DIJON MUSTARD
¼	CUP EXTRA VIRGIN OLIVE OIL
3	SCALLIONS SLICED, WHITE AND GREEN PART SEPARATED
¼	CUP DRIED CRANBERRIES, CHOPPED
1	RED OR GREEN JALAPEÑO, STEMMED, MINCED WITH THE SEEDS
2	CUPS COUSCOUS, COOKED

Marinate the drained lamb racks in the Cranberry-Teryaki Glaze overnight.

The next day, pre-heat the oven to 450° and place a heavy-bottomed pan on medium heat. Season the lamb with kosher salt and freshly ground black pepper.

Coat the pan lightly with oil and sear all sides of the rack, about 8 minutes and transfer to the oven. Roast for 5-8 additional minutes for medium rare to medium.

Meanwhile, in a large bowl, whisk together lemon juice, zest and Dijon mustard. Add olive oil and season with kosher salt and freshly ground black pepper to taste. Mix in the white part of the scallions, cranberries and jalapeños; add couscous and toss to combine.

Let the lamb rest for 5 to 8 minutes before slicing.

Place small mound of couscous salad on plates, top with lamb and garnish with scallion greens.

Serving suggestion: Serve with extra Cranberry-Teriyaki Glaze.

ABOUT MING TSAI

www.ming.com

Originally from Dayton, Ohio, Ming Tsai, a James Beard Award-winner, grew up cooking with his parents at their family-owned restaurant, Mandarin Kitchen. While pursuing a degree at Yale University, Ming spent a summer at Le Cordon Bleu in France. After graduating, Ming studied in kitchens around the globe, training in Paris under Pastry Chef Pierre Herme and in Osaka with Sushi Master Kobayashi. A graduate of Cornell University's Master's program in Hotel Administration and Hospitality Marketing, Ming has held positions in both front and back of the house at restaurants across the US. In 1998, Ming and Polly Tsai opened Blue Ginger in Wellesley, MA, and were immediately awarded 3 stars from *The Boston Globe*, and, for the last four years, Blue Ginger has been rated "2nd Most Popular Boston Restaurant" in *Zagat*.

An Emmy Award-winning host and executive producer, Ming can be seen on Public Television's "Simply Ming," now in its fourth season, as well as "Ming's Quest" and "East Meets West with Ming Tsai" on the Fine Living Network. His "Simply Ming" video podcasts feature tutorials on everything from filleting fish to decanting wine. He has authored three cookbooks and created a line of foodstuffs for Target. Ming is proud to be a national spokesperson for FAAN (the Food Allergy and Anaphylaxis Network) and a founding member of Chefs For Humanity.

- Host/Executive Producer, "Simply Ming" 2003–present
- 2004 Author *Ming's Master Recipes*
- 2003 Author *Simply Ming*
- 2002 James Beard Award, Best Chef Northeast

Q: Was your mother a good cook? What is your mother's best dish and can you duplicate it?

A: Yes, my mother is a fantastic cook. Her best dish is her salt and pepper shrimp, which I can duplicate, but the best food in the world is someone else's, especially a mom's, so when Mom makes it, it's always better.

Q: If you could meet Auguste Escoffier, what would you ask him?

A: If you were going to write your book again, how much Asian influence would there be? Do you know how to use chopsticks?

Q: If you could eat anywhere in the world, where would it be?

A: One more meal in Taipei prepared by my grandparents and their cook.

CRANBERRY-TERIYAKI LAMB RACK WITH COUSCOUS SALAD

FISH IN LEMONGRASS CARAMEL SAUCE

BY HALEY NGUYEN • SERVES 4

1	WHOLE SCALED AND GUTTED CATFISH (ABOUT 1½ POUNDS IN TOTAL WEIGHT)
2	TEASPOONS SOY SAUCE
3	TABLESPOONS FISH SAUCE
2	TABLESPOONS BROWN SUGAR
2	TABLESPOONS MOLASSES
3	TO 4 STALKS LEMONGRASS
2	TABLESPOONS CANOLA OR VEGETABLE OIL
1	TABLESPOON SHALLOT, MINCED
¾	CUP WHITE WINE OR WATER
½	TEASPOON GROUND BLACK PEPPER

Cut the fish into 3 to 4 steaks (about 1½ inches thick). Marinate with soy sauce, fish sauce, brown sugar, and molasses. Set aside for at least 30 minutes not to exceed 45 minutes.

Cut and discard the thick root end of lemongrass. Remove wilted outer leaves. Holding the lemongrass stalk upright and from the green, leafy end, grate about three-fourths of the way. You can reserve the remaining leafy end for soup or tea.

Remove the fish from the marinade, reserving the marinade.

In a deep sauté pan, heat the canola or vegetable oil on medium high heat until oil is slightly smoking. Add minced shallot and sauté for 30 seconds. Add fish and cook on high heat for 2 minutes or until slightly seared. Add white wine, black pepper, grated lemongrass and reserved marinade. Reduce heat to medium and cover the pan.

Simmer for 25 to 30 minutes, checking periodically to make sure there is some liquid remaining. If not, add ½ cup of water and continue cooking.

Uncovered and cook for another 5 minutes. Sauce should reduce to a syrup consistency.

Serving suggestion: Serve with steamed rice.

ABOUT HALEY NGUYEN

www.eastwestcooks.com

Trained at the apron strings of her grandmother, Haley learned to cook at the tender age of 10. After immigrating to the United States in 1975 with seven brothers and sisters, she obtained a Bachelor of Science degree from Indiana University in 1984. While pursuing other endeavors, her passion for food and cooking never subsided. Haley owned and operated a Vietnamese restaurant named Annam Cafe in Boulder, Colorado from 1993-1996.

Haley started her culinary teaching at the Cooking School of the Rockies in 1994. Shortly after moving to Southern California, she instigated and implemented the Asian curriculum for the Art Institute of California in Santa Monica in 1999. To complement classroom instruction, Haley leads culinary tours to Southeast Asia, one of which was aired on a Food Network segment titled "Cooking School Stories" in March 2002.

In addition, Haley conducts local market tours to Little Saigon, California, the biggest Vietnamese community outside of Vietnam. Haley also presents cooking seminars with topics including "Healthy Asian Cuisine," "How to Use Exotic Asian Ingredients" and "Asian Ingredients 101."

Haley has contributed to the Orange County Register's food sections as well as cooking web videos. She also has a Vietnamese language cooking show on Saigon TV in Orange County, which appears bi monthly on KXLA and KTSF in southern California.

Haley is currently teaching classes on ethnic cooking at Saddleback Community College and Asian cuisine at Sur la Table in Newport Beach. She lives in Irvine with her three sons and plans to open an Asian/Fusion café in March 2007. Haley will also conduct weekly cooking classes at her café on Asian cooking.

Q: What is your favorite comfort food?
A: Hot, steamy sticky rice top with simmering fish in sweet & tangy soy glazed.

Q: If not for food, where would you be now?
A: Can't really tell, but I'd be unhappy and very cranky.

Q: If you could eat anywhere in the world, where would it be?
A: Portugal, for salted fish.

CHICKEN AND BEAN STEW

CHICKEN AND BEAN STEW

BY DARA BUNJON • SERVES 4*

This recipe is a conglomerate of various dishes I have prepared from many different sources. My inspiration is Ribolitta, the Italian bean and cabbage soup where some of the beans are puréed and put them back in the pot. I like mixing dried and fresh herbs in my dishes, each having its own, distinctive flavor. While the dried are intense and earthy, the fresh herbs offer a clean fragrance that stimulates olfactory senses.

¼	CUP ALL-PURPOSE FLOUR
1	TEASPOON KOSHER SALT
1	TEASPOON FRESHLY GROUND BLACK PEPPER
2	OUNCES PANCETTA, CHOPPED
3	POUNDS SKINLESS BONELESS CHICKEN THIGHS, TRIMMED OF EXCESS FAT
2	TABLESPOONS CANOLA OIL OR OLIVE OIL
1	CUP CHOPPED ONION, MEDIUM DICE
3	LARGE GARLIC CLOVES, GRATED
1	TABLESPOON DRIED BASIL
1	TABLESPOON DRIED OREGANO
2	14½ OUNCE CANS OF DICED TOMATOES
1½	PLUS ½ CUPS CHICKEN STOCK, HOMEMADE OR LOW SODIUM
½	CUP MERLOT OR OTHER DRY RED WINE
2	15-OUNCE CANS OF CANNELLINI BEANS, RINSED AND DRAINED, SETTING ASIDE ½ CUP OF DRAINED BEANS
¼	CUP JULIENNED FRESH BASIL

Mix the flour, salt, and black pepper together.

In a large pot (Dutch oven) cook the pancetta over a medium heat until it is light brown and has rendered its fat. While the pancetta is browning, dust each piece of chicken in the flour, salt and pepper mixture. Shake off any excess flour and set aside. Remove the pancetta from the pot and drain on a paper towel.

Add the oil to the pot, raising the heat to medium high. Brown the chicken pieces in batches, moving them to a large plate when done.

Add the chopped onion and sauté, stirring with a wooden or heat-proof spatula. Once the onions become translucent, stir in the grated garlic, dried basil, and dried oregano and cook for a minute until the herbs become aromatic. Add the cooked pancetta, 2 cans of diced tomatoes with their liquid, 1½ cups of chicken stock and ½ cup of wine. Stir well. Bring to a boil, then reduce to a simmer. Add the browned chicken pieces and any liquid that has accrued on the plate.

Take the reserved ½ cup of chicken stock and the reserved ½ cup of beans and purée them together. Add this purée, plus all of the remaining whole beans, to the pot. Cover and let simmer on a medium low heat for 20 minutes.

Stir in the julienned, fresh basil just before serving.

Serve with warm, crusty bread and a simple salad.

*Note: This recipe yields leftovers. Alternatively, invite two more guests to the dinner table.

ABOUT DARA BUNJON

http:www.dara-does-it.com • http:www.diningdish.blogspot.com (see Soups, page 117)

ROAST PORK LOIN WITH POMEGRANATE, ORANGE, AND GINGER

BY JOYCE GOLDSTEIN • SERVES 6

This pork recipe has evolved over time into a cross-cultural dish. It was inspired by a grenadine-glazed pork from Roy de Groot's Feast for All Seasons. De Groot's sauce was a variation on the classic port, citrus and mustard "Cumberland" sauce the English like to serve with game. I found the pomegranate based grenadine too sweet and have substituted pomegranate molasses-giving the dish a decidedly Middle Eastern accent. I replaced the port with the less sweet and more herbaceous vermouth. The ginger and mustard add an Asian note and a bit of heat that plays nicely off the sweet and tart aspects of the pomegranate and orange. I think this recipe would undoubtedly work well with duck, squab, and even lamb.

1	5 POUND RACK OF PORK LOIN
2	LARGE CLOVES GARLIC CUT INTO SLIVERS

SPICE PASTE

2	TABLESPOONS FINELY GRATED GARLIC
2	TEASPOONS FRESHLY GRATED NUTMEG
2	TABLESPOONS CHOPPED FRESH THYME
2	TEASPOONS GRATED FRESH GINGER
2	TEASPOONS SALT
1	TEASPOON BLACK PEPPER

BASTING MIXTURE

1	CUP ORANGE JUICE
4	TABLESPOONS HONEY
4	TABLESPOONS POMEGRANATE MOLASSES

SAUCE

2	TABLESPOONS BUTTER
¼	CUP FINELY MINCED SHALLOTS

Preheat the oven to 400°. Insert slivers of garlic in between the bones of the roast. Rub the roast liberally with a paste of garlic, nutmeg, thyme, ginger, salt and pepper. Set the pork in a roasting pan and roast for about an hour or until a meat thermometer registers 140°, basting occasionally with a mixture of orange juice, pomegranate syrup and honey. Remove the pork from the oven and set aside. Keep warm until you bring the sauce to a boil.

While the pork roasts, make the sauce: In a small sauce pan over low heat, melt the butter and sauté the shallots for about 5 minutes, or until soft. Combine the pomegranate molasses, orange juice, and mustard and add to the shallots. Add the ginger, cayenne, sweet vermouth, chicken stock and the orange zest and simmer a few minutes. Add honey, salt, and pepper, and adjust the seasoning to taste. Keep the sauce warm. Slice the pork and pour the sauce over the meat.

Suggested wine: dry German Riesling or fruity young reds like Beaujolais.

Serving suggestion: Serve with sweet potatoes and sautéed greens or Brussels sprouts.

¼	CUP POMEGRANATE SYRUP
1	CUP ORANGE JUICE
2	TABLESPOONS HOT MUSTARD
2	TABLESPOONS GRATED FRESH GINGER ROOT
½	TEASPOON CAYENNE
⅓	CUP SWEET VERMOUTH
¾	CUP CHICKEN STOCK
2	TABLESPOONS GRATED ORANGE ZEST
2	TABLESPOONS HONEY
	SALT AND PEPPER

ROAST PORK LOIN WITH POMEGRANATE, ORANGE, AND GINGER

Joyce Goldstein is a consultant to the restaurant and food industries. For twelve years she was Chef/Owner of the ground-breaking Mediterranean Restaurant, Square One, in San Francisco, which received numerous and prestigious industry awards for food, wine and service. Prior to Square One, Joyce was chef of the Cafe at Chez Panisse for 3 years. She was also Visiting Executive Chef of the Wine Spectator Restaurant at the Culinary Institute of America in Napa. Joyce was voted San Francisco magazine's Chef of the Year in 1992 and received the James Beard Award for Best Chef in California for 1993. She is a Founding Board Member of Women Chefs and Restaurateurs.

Joyce is a prolific cookbook author, cooking teacher and lecturer.

Some of her cookbook titles are *The Mediterranean Kitchen, Back to Square One*—winner of both the Julia Child and James Beard Awards for Best General Cookbook of 1992, and *Kitchen Conversations*—an IACP book award nominee in 1997. Her most recent books are *Italian Slow and Savory*—IACP and Beard award nominee, *Solo Suppers, Cucina Ebraica: Flavors of the Italian Jewish Kitchen, Sephardic Flavors: Jewish Cooking of the Mediterranean, Enoteca: Simple, Delicious Food from Italian Wine Bars, Saffron Shores, Jewish Cooking of the Southern Mediterranean.*

Joyce has written numerous books for Williams-Sonoma; the most recent is *Savoring Spain and Portugal* and contributed the recipes for *Perfect Pairings*, a book by her son, Evan Goldstein. Joyce also writes Food and Wine Pairing columns for the *San Francisco Chronicle.*

Q: What is your favorite comfort food?
A: Soft polenta or farro with butter and corn

Q: If you were condemned to die, what would be your last meal?
A: Spaghetti alla Carbonara

Q: If you could eat anywhere in the world, where would it be?
A: Italy, because the food is so varied from region to region. After that Turkey or Spain.

Q: Was your mother a good cook? What is your mother's best dish and can you duplicate it?
A: No one in my family was a good cook. I learned to cook in self defense. I knew there was good food out there (I had dined in many fine restaurants). I knew that if I wanted to eat that well, I'd have to learn how to cook. I am self-taught.

CHICKEN WITH SUNCHOKES, GARLIC, CAPERS, AND WHITE WINE

BY ERIC CROWLEY • SERVES 4

4	CHICKEN BREASTS, BONELESS AND SKINLESS
2	TABLESPOONS PLUS 2 TABLESPOONS OLIVE OIL
	SALT AND FRESHLY GROUND BLACK PEPPER
½	CUP ALL-PURPOSE FLOUR, FOR DREDGING
¼	CUP PLUS ¼ CUP WHITE WINE
¾	POUND SUNCHOKES, SCRUBBED AND SLICED
4	CLOVES GARLIC, SLICED THINLY
¼	CUP CAPERS, DRAINED AND CHOPPED
½	CUP CHICKEN STOCK OR BROTH

Lightly pound the chicken breasts until they are of uniform thickness. Place the chicken on a plate and set aside.

Heat a sauté pan or skillet over medium heat. Make sure that the pan is large enough to hold the chicken without crowding. Add just enough oil to coat the bottom of the pan well (approximately 2 tablespoons).

While the oil is heating, season the chicken with salt and pepper. Spread the flour in a baking dish or similar container. Coat both sides of the chicken in the flour, patting off the excess. Place the chicken in the pan and sauté until the chicken is golden brown on both sides, about 2 to 4 minutes per side.

Remove the chicken from the pan and place it in a clean bowl and set aside. Pour off any excess oil in the pan and add ¼ cup of wine. Scrape any browned bits from the bottom of the pan, pouring everything into the bowl holding the reserved chicken.

Return the pan to the heat and add enough oil to coat the bottom (approximately 2 tablespoons). Add the sunchokes and sauté, stirring frequently for about 3 to 5 minutes. Season while cooking with a pinch of salt and pepper.

Add the garlic slices and sauté for 2 minutes. Add the remaining wine and broth or stock. Return the chicken and any juices to the pan. Lower the heat to simmer, cover, and cook for 4 minutes.

Uncover the pan and check for doneness. If the chicken is no longer pink inside, it is done. Add the capers. Taste the sauce and season to taste with salt and pepper. If the sauce is too thick, thin it with more stock or water.

Place the chicken on warm plates and pour the sauce over top. Serve.

Suggested wine: Chardonnay or Champagne.

Serving suggestions: This dish goes well with sautéed spinach and mashed potatoes; sautéed zucchini, red bell peppers and pasta; roasted pumpkin or acorn squash and polenta.

ABOUT ERIC CROWLEY

www.culinaryclassroom.com

Chef Eric has been a professional chef for ten years, a chef instructor for eight years and the owner/chef instructor at Chef Eric's Culinary Classroom for 4 years. Chef Eric graduated with honors from the Culinary Institute of America in Hyde Park, New York. European-trained, he worked with Chef José Munisa at Via Veneto, Barcelona's longest-running 5 Star restaurant, as well as with Chef Joseph Russwürm at Munich's Hotel Kempinski, another 5 Star establishment.

Chef Eric worked with Patina Catering—of the famed Patina Restaurant Group—supervising catering of corporate and personal events from an intimate 4-person lunch or dinner to a boisterous crowd of 2,000 for lunch, dinner or just appetizers. He has cooked meals for presidential candidates, vice presidents, show business executives, celebrities, and numerous personal clients. He has also prepared elaborate private dinners and specialty meals for country club and consulate guests.

In addition to donating thousands of dollars worth of cooking classes each year to various Los Angeles schools and charities, Chef Eric is a C-Cap program judge and scholarship sponsor (Career Through the Culinary Arts). He is also a mentor for the Culinary Institute of America (CIA) and hosts open houses for potential CIA students.

Since 1999, Chef Eric has taught professional and recreational cooking classes to thousands of students. Many of whom are successful restaurant owners, chefs, caterers and personal chefs. His cooking, catering, and teaching career is studded with accolades from students, clients, and employers. His love of gourmet food, cooking, and teaching is apparent.

Q: If you could eat anywhere in the world, where would it be?

A: On a beach in Hawaii with my lovely wife. I love the fresh fish, fruits and vegetables in Hawaii and everything seems to taste better there.

Q: What food could I live without and why?

A: I could live without calves' brains. I cleaned enough of them when I worked at Via Veneto in Barcelona, Spain and I have no desire to eat them again.

Q: Was your mother a good cook? What is your mother's best dish and can you duplicate it?

A: Yes, her talents eventually led me to my career as a chef. With all of the excellent meals she has made, I have to say it is her Chow Yoke, one of her specialties. This is a Chinese-style fried beef that is, as with all of her Asian Cuisine, fantastic. I can duplicate it, but it is never quite the same as when she makes it.

RISOTTO CON CERVO

BY ARIANE DAGUIN • SERVES 6

This substantial main course marries slowly-simmered venison, perfumed with rosemary and Barolo wine, with creamy risotto. For lovers of game and Italian food, it's an incomparable match. Before serving, a generous spoonful of the tender meat and rich sauce is spooned on top of the risotto.

½   CUP DRIED PORCINI MUSHROOMS

¼   CUP PLUS ¼ CUP OLIVE OIL

1   ONION, MINCED (RESERVE 2
       TABLESPOONS)

½   CUP MINCED PANCETTA OR BACON
       SALT AND FRESHLY GROUND
       BLACK PEPPER TO TASTE

2   POUNDS VENISON LEG OR
       SHOULDER, WELL TRIMMED,
       SILVER SKIN REMOVED, AND CUT
       INTO 1-INCH CUBES

2   BAY LEAVES

1   SPRIG FRESH ROSEMARY PLUS A
       FEW SMALL SPRIGS TO GARNISH,
       IF DESIRED

2   WHOLE CLOVES

½   CUP DRY RED WINE, PREFERABLY
       BAROLO

2   TABLESPOONS TOMATO PASTE

6   CUPS PLUS 2 CUPS CHICKEN
       STOCK

1   SHALLOT, MINCED

2   CUPS ARBORIO RICE

½   CUP DRY WHITE WINE

2   TABLESPOONS UNSALTED BUTTER,
       CUT INTO SMALL PIECES

½   CUP FRESHLY GRATED
       PARMIGIANO-REGGIANO

Soak porcini in 2 cups of hot water until softened, about 20 minutes. Meanwhile, heat ¼ cup of the olive oil in a large casserole over medium-high heat. Add all but 2 tablespoons of the onions and all of the pancetta or bacon to the pan, and sauté until golden, about 8 minutes. Season lightly with salt and pepper, add the venison, and cook until all the meat liquids have evaporated, about 15 minutes.

Pick out the hydrated porcini and chop them coarsely, reserving the liquid except for the last 2 tablespoons of gritty sediment. Add porcini to casserole, along with bay leaves, one sprig of rosemary, cloves, and red wine, and cook, stirring, for 5 minutes, until the wine has nearly evaporated. Stir in tomato paste and seasoning lightly with salt and pepper.

Add 2 cups of chicken stock and reserved mushroom liquid slowly. Bring to a boil, then reduce heat to medium-low. Simmer, partially covered until meat is tender, and the sauce is thickened, about 1½ hours. Remove bay leaves and rosemary, adjust seasoning, and set aside. Recipe may be made several days in advance, covered, and refrigerated. Warm before continuing.

Heat the remaining 6 cups of chicken stock and keep warm. Heat the remaining ¼ cup of olive oil in a medium casserole over medium-high heat. Add the reserved 2 tablespoons of onion and the shallot, and sauté until golden. Stir in rice, turning to coat with oil. Pour in white wine, stir well, and add ½ cup of the hot stock, and season with about a teaspoon of salt. Cook, stirring constantly, until all liquid has been absorbed.

Stir in half of the venison and sauce. Continue to add hot stock in small batches, and cook until each successive batch has been absorbed, stirring constantly, until rice mixture is creamy and al dente. Remove from heat, stir in butter and cheese, and season with pepper. Ladle risotto onto 6 large plates. Spoon the remaining venison and sauce over each portion, add a small sprig of rosemary, and serve.

Note: By slowly adding hot liquid to risotto, the starchy outer coat of each grain of Arborio rice melts into the broth and thickens it. What remains in a small firm center.

Add the liquid in small amounts, stir pan thoroughly and continuously, and adjust the heat to keep it brisk, but not too high, so the liquid evaporates slowly enough to soften the rice without making it pasty. Usually, this takes about 30 minutes.

Q: If you could meet Auguste Escoffier, what would you ask him?
A: How did he come up with the brilliant idea for Tournedos Rossini (steak topped with Foie Gras)? Was it really his idea or was it Rossini's?

Q: If you were condemned to die, what would be your last meal?
A: Lièvre à La Royale (Hare deboned, stuffed with foie gras & truffles and cooked for 3 days).

Q: If you could eat anywhere in the world, where would it be?
A: In the spring: at my godfather's Zizou, eating a fresh baby fava bean soup. In December: in Bouzigues, eating a platter of oysters and mussels from L'étang de Thau. In October: at Ramouneda's, a woodcock "à la ficelle" (cooked on a string in the fireplace). In February: in Jurançon, a dry cured ham from the Pyréneés black pig.

ABOUT ARIANE DAGUIN

www.dartagnan.com

Ariane Daguin was born into a world of great food. Her father, André Daguin, chef-owner of the Hotel de France in Auch, Gascony, is famous throughout France for his artistry with foie gras and other Gascon specialties. Ariane was expert at deboning ducks, rendering duck fat, preparing terrines and cooking the game birds her grandfather hunted by the time she was ten.

While a career in food might have seemed natural, Ariane pursued an academic degree at Columbia University. While working part-time for a New York pâté producer, Ariane had the opportunity to market the first domestically produced foie gras. She and George Faison, a co-worker and fellow grad student, pooled their resources to launch D'Artagnan.

According to Danny Meyer (owner of Union Square Café and other top New York restaurants), "Everyone in the food world knows how influential D'Artagnan has been in almost single-handedly bringing great game and foie gras to chefs in America."

In 2005, D'Artagnan celebrated its twentieth anniversary. At the same time, Ariane acquired George's share of the company to become sole owner.

Ariane is founding president of Les Nouvelles Mères Cuisinières and active in Les Dames d'Escoffier, The American Institute of Wine & Food, Women Chefs and Restaurateurs, La Chaîne des Rôtisseurs and the Conseil du Commerce Extérieur de la France. In 2005, Ariane received the "Lifetime Achievement Award" from *Bon Appetit* Magazine, an award previously bestowed upon Julia Child and James Beard. In 2006, Ariane was awarded the French Legion of Honor.

She lives in New York City with her daughter Alix.

ACHIEVEMENTS

- 2006 French Legion of Honor
- 2005 *Bon Appetit* Lifetime Achievement Award

RISOTTO CON CERVO

GRILLED SALMON FILLETS WITH LIME GINGER BUTTER

GRILLED SALMON FILLETS WITH LIME GINGER BUTTER

BY JENNIFER BUSHMAN • SERVES 4

1	TEASPOON WHOLE CORIANDER SEED
1	TEASPOON WHOLE FENNEL SEED
1	TEASPOON FINELY GRATED FRESH GINGER
1	TEASPOON PAPRIKA
1	TABLESPOON KOSHER SALT
⅛	TEASPOON CAYENNE PEPPER
4	6-OUNCE SALMON FILLETS
4	TABLESPOONS BUTTER
1	TEASPOON LIME ZEST, FINELY ZESTED
1	TABLESPOON LIME JUICE
2	TEASPOONS CHOPPED FRESH CILANTRO
	SALT AND FRESHLY GROUND BLACK PEPPER
2	TABLESPOONS OLIVE OIL

Preheat the grill for 10 minutes to medium high heat. Clean and season grill.

Toast the whole coriander and fennel seeds in a small skillet over medium heat for 1 to 2 minutes, until fragrant. Spoon the seeds from the skillet into a spice grinder and grind to a coarse powder. Place in a small bowl and stir in the grated ginger, paprika, kosher salt, and cayenne pepper.

Lightly sprinkle the dry rub evenly over the salmon fillets and marinate 15 minutes at room temperature. Reserve any remaining rub for another use.

In a small saucepan melt butter. Remove from the heat and add lime zest, lime juice, and cilantro. Season to taste with salt and freshly ground pepper.

Gently brush the seasoned salmon fillets with olive oil. Place on the preheated grill, skin side down and grill, without moving, for 4 minutes.

Using a fish or grill spatula, gently turn the fillets over and baste with lime/cilantro butter. Continue grilling, another 4 minutes. Fillets will be a beautiful medium rare. Cook a minute or two longer on both sides if you like your salmon well done. Remove the fillets from grill, baste again with the flavored butter, and serve warm.

Suggested wine: Oregon Pinot Noir or a refreshing Sauvignon Blanc.

Note: This salmon recipe is easy to prepare and simply delicious. Serve with a salad of mixed greens, sliced bell pepper, olives, and a lime vinaigrette to perpetuate the citrus flavor.

ABOUT JENNIFER BUSHMAN

www.kitchencoach.com

At a time when "sit down dinner" means ordering at the take out counter or going through the drive thru, the very idea of whipping up something healthy for dinner at home is enough to make most of us dive for the mini-van keys.

But not if you have encountered Jennifer Bushman, Kitchen Coach™. Bushman's culinary drive springs from her childhood filled with great cooks. Her mother and grandmother both encouraged her natural curiosity in the kitchen. By the age of 8, she was fine tuning her grandmother's cookie recipes. Those recipes were used to start her first company, Jennifer's Cookies. Bushman's entrepreneurial approach led her from cookie baker to full time culinary professional. Jennifer was the founder of Nothing to It Culinary Center in Reno, Nevada. She is the National Culinary Spokesperson for the American Heart Association, and is a frequent keynote speaker for the Go Red for Women fund raising luncheons throughout the west. She teaches cooking classes though out the country and has been nominated for the IACP "Cooking School of the Year" award, the Julia Child "Best in Media" award, as well as the James Beard Foundation "Broadcast Media" award.

ACHIEVEMENTS

- 2004 *Kitchen Coach Weeknight Cooking* (John Wiley and sons)
- 2005 *Kitchen Coach Weekend Cooking* (John Wiley and sons)
- 2006 *Kitchen Coach Family Meals* (John Wiley and sons)

Q: What is your favorite family recipe?

A: My Grandfathers buttermilk pancakes, he made them every Saturday morning for breakfast with hot maple syrup and a blend of freshly chopped strawberries and a small amount of sour cream.

Q: What put you on the culinary career path?

A: The foundation came from my grandmother. She taught me the importance of gathering in the kitchen. From the family meal, to the most elaborate celebration, all of the things that I learned and loved about the people in my family came from the kitchen. It is why I work so hard to motivate families to gather and cook together.

Q: If you could eat anywhere in the world, where would it be?

A: I would choose to eat at my Grandmother's table on a Friday night. She passed away ten years ago this summer. Every Friday night she made the most incredible pot roast with carmelized potatoes, carrots and shallots.

SWEET TEA CURED PORK RACK

BY JOHN FLEER • SERVES 10

1   5-POUND RACK OF PORK LOIN,
       TRIMMED OF FAT AND SINEW

BRINE

1   QUART BREWED TEA, DOUBLE
       STRENGTH
1   ZESTED LEMON, QUARTERED
1   CUP SUGAR
½   CUP KOSHER SALT
1   QUART ICE WATER

RUB

½   CUP LEMON ZEST (SAVE ONE
       ZESTED LEMON FOR THE BRINE)
¼   CUP FINELY CHOPPED FRESH MINT
       LEAVES
2   TABLESPOONS FINELY CHOPPED
       FRESH THYME
2   TABLESPOONS FINELY CHOPPED
       TEA LEAVES

For the brine, combine all of the ingredients except the ice water and simmer for 5 minutes or until salt and sugar are completely dissolved. Pour in the ice water and cool brine completely. Submerge pork rack in brine for 48 hours.

After pork has brined, remove to a wire rack. For the dry rub, combine lemon zest, mint, thyme and tea leaves together in a small bowl. Rub the herb/tea mixture over the top sides of the pork rack. Let the meat sit for one hour in the refrigerator before roasting.

Preheat the oven to 350°.

While still on the wire rack, roast pork rack in a 350° oven for 1 hour. Using a meat thermometer check the internal temperature of the pork rack. The pork should have a temperature of 135°. Continue roasting until pork has reached this temperature. The total roasting time is approximately 1 to 1½ hours.

Let rest for 5 minutes before slicing. Slice off individual chops.

ABOUT JOHN FLEER

www.blackberryfarm.com

As a leader of the new guard of Southern chefs, John Fleer continues to merge traditional southern ingredients and methods with innovative techniques to create magical renditions of Southern fare. Foothills Cuisine, Fleer's unique style, has found its way in to the pages of *Food & Wine, Gourmet*, and *Bon Appétit*. He has also appeared in television programs that include The Food Network's "Ready, Set Cook," "Off the Menu" from Turner South, "Great country Inns" and "Great Chefs of the South." He was selected as one of the "Rising Stars of the 21st Century" by the James Beard Foundation. When the Zagat Survey honored Blackberry Farm naming it #1 Small Hotel in America for 2003 and 2004, Fleer's "Foothills Cuisine" was described as "incredible" and rated #2 for Hotel Dining in America. Marked with success, Chef Fleer's culinary career began as a way to pay for graduate school in North Carolina. Not able to shake his life's passion, Fleer enrolled at the Culinary Institute of America. Following a fellowship at the one of the CIA's restaurants and a stint as Mary Tyler Moore's personal chef, Fleer joined Blackberry Farm in 1992. Under Fleer's culinary direction Blackberry Farm recently received the honor of becoming a Relais Gourmand.

Q: What is your favorite comfort food?
A: Mashed potatoes and oxtail.

Q: If you could eat anywhere in the world, where would it be?
A: Mugaritz (Spain).

Q: What food could you live without and why?
A: Steak, because there is much more interesting food in the world.

SWEET TEA CURED PORK RACK

THAI CURRY SEA SCALLOPS

BY CHRISTINE KEFF • SERVES 4

2	TABLESPOONS PEANUT OIL OR CANOLA OIL
20	LARGE SEA SCALLOPS
	SALT AND BLACK PEPPER
3	TABLESPOONS THAI CURRY PASTE (SEE PAGE 268)
1½	CUPS COCONUT MILK
1	TABLESPOON LIME JUICE
1	TABLESPOON FISH SAUCE

Place peanut oil in a large non-stick skillet. Heat to smoking. Remove from flame and quickly add scallops to pan, one by one. Season with salt and pepper. Return to flame and sear scallops on one side, then the other. Process should take approximately 4-5 minutes; scallops will be medium rare

Transfer scallops to a warm platter and discard extra oil from pan. Add Thai Curry Paste and sauté briefly. Add coconut milk and continue to simmer until sauce is thick enough to coat a spoon. Add lime juice and fish sauce. Strain through a fine sieve, then pour sauce over scallops and serve.

Suggested wine: Fruit forward Pinot Noir.

ABOUT CHRISTINE KEFF
www.flyingfishseattle.com
(see Salads, page 136)

BEEF BRAISED WITH BLACK SOYBEAN MISO

BY HIROKO SHIMBO • SERVES 4

Cooking a large cut of beef or other such meats has not been part of traditional Japanese cooking. Even today, and except for Japanese-style steak preparations, most beef dishes still call for thinly sliced beef—as in sukiyaki and shabu-shabu. Now that the price of beef in Japan is coming down, and the ovens in most households are larger, beef can be enjoyed in many different ways. It can be prepared in a typically Western fashion—a big chunk of meat braised in the oven—but of course, with a Japanese twist.

When I prepare such beef dishes, I love to flavor them with black soybean miso (kuro-daizu miso) and excellent quality akasake mirin. Both are indispensable ingredients in my kitchen. Finely grated ginger and garlic added to the braising liquid produce a wonderful texture and flavor in this hearty winter dish.

2	TABLESPOONS KOSHER SALT
3	POUNDS BEEF CHUCK, BONELESS
10	SLICES FRESH GINGER
1½	CUPS SAKE
1	CUP WATER
1	CUP AKASAKE MIRIN OR REGULAR MIRIN (SWEET JAPANESE COOKING WINE)
1½	TABLESPOONS KURO-DAIZU MISO (BLACK SOYBEAN MISO)
1	TABLESPOON FINELY GRATED FRESH GINGER
1	TABLESPOON FINELY GRATED GARLIC
1	TO 2 TABLESPOON SWEETENED BEMIMOSU (HONEY-SWEETENED PURPLE SWEET POTATO VINEGAR) OR OTHER VINEGAR BLENDED WITH HONEY TO TASTE

Salt the beef and refrigerate overnight

Rinse the beef to remove the salt. Drain the beef and wipe dry with a paper towel. In a pot large enough to hold the beef, add the ginger slices, sake, water and mirin. Bring the liquid to a simmer and add the beef.

Cover the pot with a tight heavy lid and transfer it to a heated oven (300°). Cook the beef for 2½ hours. Remove the pot from the oven and let cool. Refrigerate the beef and cooking liquid overnight.

Remove the solidified fat from the cooking liquid. Trim any fat from the beef and cut it into 2½" x 2" x 1" pieces.

Return the cooking liquid to a pot and bring it to a simmer. Add the beef and cook, covered, until the beef is heated through. Add the miso, grated ginger and garlic and cook 15 minutes. Transfer the beef to an oven-proof container and keep it warm in the oven. Reduce the cooking liquid. Add the sweetened Benimosu or honey and vinegar mixture to the cooking liquid to taste.

Serving suggestions: Arrange an individual portion of beef on top of cooked collard greens. Spoon the reduced cooking liquid over the beef. Garnish with sweet potato French fries.

ABOUT HIROKO SHIMBO

www.hirokoskitchen.com www.nymtc.com

Hiroko Shimbo, a recognized authority on Japanese cuisine, consults for restaurants and food companies. She offers professional consulting services and cooking classes at schools, food companies and restaurants throughout the United States and Europe. Hiroko began her business, Hiroko's Kitchen, in her native Japan in 1989 offering lectures and cooking instruction to the foreign community in Tokyo. Since 1999 her base of operation has been New York City. Hiroko also writes cookbooks and food articles for consumer and professional magazines including *Saveur* and *National Culinary Review.*

Hiroko's award-winning, best selling cookbook *The Japanese Kitchen* was published in 2000. This comprehensive book, already the standard English language work on Japanese cuisine, is designed to demystify Japanese cooking for Western cooks using locally available ingredients. *The Japanese Kitchen* has been translated and is being sold throughout the Spanish speaking world.

Hiroko's next major book, *The Sushi Experience,* was published in 2006. The lavishly illustrated book is the most comprehensive treatment of sushi ever published in English. It presents the history and cultural associations of sushi, sushi restaurant dining tips and etiquette, and complete instruction on the ingredients, techniques and recipes of this world cuisine.

Hiroko appears on radio and television throughout the United States. She is also currently working as culinary consultant for the newly opened Taneko Japanese Tavern restaurant in Phoenix, Arizona, intended to become a nation-wide chain. Hiroko is a member of the International Association of Culinary Professionals and the Women's Chef and Restaurateurs.

ACHIEVEMENTS

- 2006 *The Sushi Experience* (Alfred A. Knopf)
- 2000 *The Japanese Kitchen: 250 Recipes in a traditional spirit* (Harvard Common Press)
- Victory Garden (PBS television series; several appearances)

Q: What is your favorite comfort food?

A: There is no specific dish that comes to mind. What I favor are foods prepared using fresh seasonal ingredients and simple cooking techniques which highlight and does not mask the flavor of these wonderful gifts of nature. Any dish—vegetable, seafood, meat—that brings a sense of season and simplicity is a comfort food for me.

BEEF BRAISED WITH BLACK SOYBEAN MISO

Q: What put you on the culinary career path?
A: Love of cooking and eating well taught to me by my most respected teacher, my mother. At age 79 she is still the person who gives me guidance and advice on all cooking matters. This has led to an insatiable curiosity to learn everything I can about culinary culture—the history, traditions and people.

Q: Was your mother a good cook? What is your mother's best dish and can you duplicate it?
A: She is a terrific cook. It is hard to select one preparation as the best dish, since I consider all of her cooking to be "best." She inspired in me the respect for fresh seasonal ingredients prepared with minimal cooking. As my teacher, I have worked very hard to master all of the techniques and recipes that I learned—and still learn—from her. A simple perfectly grilled fish, sashimi prepared from a wonderful whole fish, special very seasonal but simple dishes such as steamed rice with autumn chestnuts, and typical Japanese home-style preparations like curry-rice all come to mind.

ROASTED BALSAMIC-GLAZED CHICKEN

BY REGGIE SOUTHERLAND • SERVES 4

BRINE (OPTIONAL)

5	QUARTS WATER
½	CUP COARSE OR SEA SALT
¼	CUP SUGAR

ROASTING

1	LARGE LEMON
¼	CUP BALSAMIC VINEGAR
¼	CUP EXTRA-VIRGIN OLIVE OIL
2	TEASPOONS SALT
1	TEASPOON FRESHLY GROUND BLACK PEPPER
3	TABLESPOONS HERBS DE PROVENCE
1	5- TO 6-POUND ROASTING CHICKEN (BRINED OPTIONAL)
4	CLOVES PLUS 4 CLOVES GARLIC
4	SPRIGS ROSEMARY
2	WHITE ONIONS, THICKLY SLICED
2	FENNEL BULBS, SLICED IN HALF LENGTHWISE
¼	CUP CHICKEN STOCK

Brining: In a 6-quart container combine water, salt and sugar. Make sure the sugar and salt have dissolved. Place chicken in the cool or room temperature solution making sure it's completely submerged. Cover and place in refrigerator for six hours or overnight.

Roasting the chicken: Preheat the oven to 350°. Using a fine zester or grater, zest the whole lemon. Then cut the lemon in half and juice. Do not discard the fruit.

Combine the vinegar, oil, salt, pepper, Herbs de Provence, lemon juice and lemon zest in a bowl, whisking until emulsified, to make a marinade.

Thinly slice four garlic cloves. Lift the skin on the breast of the chicken and place the sliced garlic underneath. Pour the marinade over and in the chicken, making sure to completely coat the bird.

Insert the reserved squeezed lemons, along with the rosemary and remaining four garlic cloves into the cavity.

Layer the onion slices in the roasting pan. They will act as a roasting rack for the chicken. Place the chicken on top of the onions. Place the fennel halves cut side down around the chicken. Add ¼ cup of chicken stock to the pan.

Put the chicken in the oven. Immediately reduce the temperature to 300° and roast for 1 to 1½ hours, basting occasionally. This chicken gets very dark when roasting. If you're concerned about burning, tent with foil; however be sure to remove it for the last 15 minutes of cooking.

Note: This chicken is especially good if you have the time to brine the chicken ahead of time. Brining the chicken makes it incredibly moist and succulent.

Serving suggestions: Serve with mashed sweet potatoes and a vegetable salad made with steamed green beans, peas and asparagus.

A really refreshing and unique beverage to go with this meal is what I call a Lemon Madres. I mimic the flavors found in the marinade to make light but potent cocktail.

In a tumbler, add crushed ice and a fresh sprig of rosemary that has been rubbed gently between your hands (to release it's aroma). Pour 2 ounces of brandy, 4 ounces of sparkling lemon soda (not Sprite), a squeeze of fresh lemon and, for added garnish, a slice of lemon. Stir and serve.

ABOUT REGGIE SOUTHERLAND

In 2005, Reggie opened the Comfort Café for his long-time friend Jackie Joniec, in the trendy L.A. neighborhood of Silver Lake. He not only designed and created the simple yet exquisite menu, but he also introduced his line of mouthwatering baked goods. And Los Angeles foodies noticed! His clients include some of Hollywood's biggest stars, and he's treated them like family… catering weddings, corporate events, premieres, and those exclusive parties.

Reggie was born and raised in good old New York City where he began cooking at the age of 11. His mother (bless her heart) worked long hours so he had to cook for his sister after school (he attended The American Academy for the Dramatic Arts). He recalls, "I was really influenced by Julia Child 'The French Chef' and watched it intently even though I never made anything she cooked! I started baking for school functions and family celebrations. While in college (New York City's Hunter College where he studied theatre, theatrical design, and photography) I really became interested in baking. I worked at a local Baskin-Robbins, decorating their ice cream cakes. I wanted to go to culinary school for pastry arts, but when I inquired about the tuition, I was informed that it would cost about $18,000.00. Well, I nearly took a heart attack! So, I read a lot of books, watched every cooking show I could and taught myself through trial and a lot of error!"

- 2005 "The Next Food Network Star," Season 3 (Food Network Television)

Q: What is your favorite comfort food?

A: Well that's easy—chicken potpie! I make the whole pie from scratch, crust and all! I cannot tell you how many I have made over the years and I believe I have a DAMN good recipe. I started making it in my twenties—it became a Wednesday special at the café I worked in and I've made it on national television (I've gotten a lot of mileage out of this recipe). This is a dish that I've developed and changed over the years and one that I make whenever I need to feel really good.

Q: What put you on the culinary career path?

A: It all started for me when I was about eleven years old, I watched The French Chef with Julia Child and I was hooked. Julia Child introduced me to food as a form of art and great fun while doing it.

Q: If you were condemned to die, what would be your last meal?

A: One of my absolute favorite meals comes from a restaurant in New York City (where I'm originally from) called Café Rosso. To my great sadness the café closed in the fall of 2005 but the food there was lovely, clean and beautiful.

I would start with a Malbec or Syrah. The salad, a warm crusted goat cheese with frisée, pancetta, roasted potatoes, and tomatoes in light mustard vinaigrette—perfect! I would then move on to the warm white beans with sausage. For an entrée it would have to be the bone-in crusted veal chop (pounded very thin) on a bed of lightly dressed arugula and tomatoes, and for dessert—Lemoncello with a fruit sorbet. Flawless!

SUGARCANE BARBEQUE'D DUCK

BY NORMAN VAN AKEN • SERVES 6

3   DOUBLE DUCK BREASTS, CUT IN
      HALF AND TRIMMED (YOU CAN
      ASK YOUR BUTCHER TO DO
      THIS)
1   RECIPE SUGARCANE MARINADE
      (SEE PAGE 267)
      KOSHER SALT
      FRESHLY TOASTED GROUND
      BLACK PEPPERCORNS, TO TASTE

With a sharp knife, score the skin of the duck breasts in a criss-cross fashion. Put them in a large re-sealable plastic bag and saturate each breast in the marinade. Refrigerate overnight.

Prepare a medium-hot grill. When the coals are ready, lightly oil the grill rods. Remove the duck from the marinade, allowing the excess liquid to fall away. Place the duck, skin side down, on the grill. Sear over direct heat. Be careful, as dripping fat may cause the fire to flare. Grill for 6 minutes.

Flip the breasts over and grill an additional 7 or 8 minutes with indirect heat, or until they are medium-rare in the center. (If your grill is too hot you might want to finish off the breasts in a 350° oven.) Allow the breasts to rest a few minutes before slicing them.

ABOUT NORMAN VAN AKEN

www.normans.com

The Forerunner of the culinary fusion movement, Norman Van Aken founded a visionary way of cooking called New World Cuisine, giving meaning to an entire region of America. Presenting an approach that embodies the essence of this country and its dynamic ethnic mix, Van Aken melds the exotic ingredients and rich cultural heritages of Latin America, the Caribbean, the southern United States and even touches of Asia. Serving as the catalyst for a new culinary paradigm, Van Aken has earned a place as one of America's greatest chefs.

Q: If you could meet Auguste Escoffier, what would you ask him?
A: Feeling a little woozy? Food sure has changed in the world, eh...

Q: If not for food, where would you be now?
A: Still in Key West, but with a bit less stuff! As long as I have Janet and Justin, it's all fine.

Q: What is your favorite family recipe?
A: Mama's Strawberry Jam.

Q: Was your mother a good cook?
A: She was a wonderful cook but she worked so hard in the restaurants she had little time for it.

TERIYAKI-GRILLED AHI WITH WASABI-DAIKON VINAIGRETTE

BY ROY YAMAGUCHI • SERVES 4

TERIYAKI MARINADE

(THIS CAN BE MADE AND REFRIGERATED FOR MONTHS)

½ CUP SOY SAUCE

½ CUP SUGAR

2 TABLESPOONS MINCED SCALLIONS (INCLUDING THE GREEN PARTS)

1 TABLESPOON GRATED GARLIC

1 TABLESPOON FINELY GRATED FRESH GINGER

4 AHI FILLETS (ABOUT 7 OUNCES EACH)

WASABI-DAIKON VINAIGRETTE

6 TABLESPOONS SOY SAUCE

6 TABLESPOON RICE VINEGAR SEASONED OR UNSEASONED

¼ CUP GRATED MAUI OR OTHER SWEET WHITE ONION

2 TABLESPOONS FRESH OGO SEAWEED OR RECONSTITUTED WAKAME*

2 TABLESPOONS WASABI PASTE

¼ CUP GRATED DAIKON

To prepare the marinade: Combine the soy sauce, sugar, scallions, garlic & ginger in a saucepan and bring to a boil. Cool and refrigerate overnight before using.

Prepare a medium-hot fire in a charcoal grill or preheat a gas grill to 450°.

Transfer marinade to a shallow, glass baking dish and add the fish. Let marinate for 10 minutes, turning once.

To prepare the vinaigrette: While the fish is marinating, prepare the vinaigrette. Combine soy sauce, rice vinegar, onion, ogo (or wakame), wasabi paste and daikon together in a mixing bowl.

Remove the fish from the marinade and grill for about 2 minutes on each side, or until a desired doneness is reached. Transfer to warmed plates and spoon the vinaigrette around the fish.

Recommended wine: Gunderloch "Rheinhessen" Riesling 2003.

*Note: Wakame is dried seaweed, reconstitute per instructions on the package.

Q: What is your favorite comfort food?
A: Ramen.

Q: What put you on the culinary career path?
A: Meeting girls in Home-Ec class.

Q: Was your mother a good cook? What is your mother's best dish and can you duplicate it?
A: Not bad. Her best dish is Green Beans with Pork, Miso & Eggs. No, I can't duplicate it. A mother's recipe with so much heart and love can never be duplicated.

ABOUT ROY YAMAGUCHI

www.roysrestaurant.com

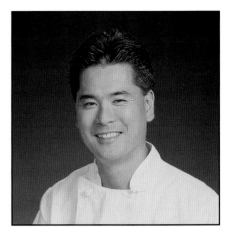

Based on childhood memories of Hawaii, Roy invented "Hawaiian Fusion© Cuisine," a combination of exotic flavors and spices mixed with the freshest of local ingredients, always with an emphasis on seafood.

Born in Tokyo, Yamaguchi vividly recalls visits with his grandparents to Maui, where he had his first tastes of fish, crab, octopus and lobster. He graduated the Culinary Institute of America in New York, where, after several years of intense training, he became a "Master Chef."

Thoroughly imbued by this discipline, Roy tackled his first experience as executive chef at Le Serene in Los Angeles in 1979, followed by a few memorable months at Michael's in Santa Monica, working for California Cuisine originator Michael McCarty. In 1984 he opened his own restaurant in Los Angeles called 385 North.

The desire to further expand his culinary horizons while getting closer to his roots led Yamaguchi to move to Hawaii in 1988 and open Roy's.

Soon after the original Roy's opened in Honolulu, *Food & Wine* dubbed it the "crown jewel of Honolulu's East-West eateries," and it was named one of Conde Nast Traveler's "Top 50." *Gourmet* acknowledged Yamaguchi as "the father of modern East-West cooking" while the *New York Times* described him as "the Wolfgang Puck of the Pacific."

Yamaguchi is now regarded as a pioneer who mastered a distinctive style, which brought his cooking to the forefront of contemporary gastronomy. There are now 34 Roy's, including 25 in the Continental US, 6 in Hawaii, 2 in Japan and 1 in Guam.

ACHIEVEMENTS

- James Beard "Best Pacific Northwest Chef" award
- Six seasons of the PBS-TV show "Hawaii Cooks with Roy Yamaguchi"
- 2005 *Roy's Fish & Seafood: Recipes from the Pacific Rim* cookbook
- 2003 *Hawaii Cooks: Flavors From Roy's Pacific Rim Kitchen* cookbook
- 1995 *Roy's Feasts from Hawaii* cookbook

ROY'S

Vegetables/Vegetarian

RISOTTO PRIMAVERA

BY MIRIAM BRICKMAN • SERVES 2*

3	TO 4 CUPS CHICKEN OR VEGETABLE STOCK
3	TABLESPOONS BUTTER
1	SMALL ONION, FINELY CHOPPED
1	CUP Arborio RICE
½	CUP DRY WHITE WINE
1	TABLESPOON SMALL DICED RED PEPPER
1	TABLESPOON SMALL DICED ZUCCHINI WITH SKIN ON
1	TABLESPOON CHOPPED CHIVES
1	TABLESPOON SMALL DICED CARROT
1	TABLESPOON TINY ASPARAGUS TIPS
2	TABLESPOONS BUTTER
⅓	CUP FINELY GRATED Parmigiano-Reggiano CHEESE

Heat the stock. In a 2-quart heavy pan, melt the butter, add the onion and allow to cook until the onion is translucent. Using moderate heat, add the dry rice, mixing with a spoon until the rice is well covered with butter. Add the wine and keep stirring, allowing the wine to evaporate slowly.

When the wine has evaporated, begin adding the stock in small amounts, ½ cup at a time, stirring frequently. Allow the stock to be absorbed by the rice before adding more stock.

Before adding the last ½ cup of stock, taste to see if there is some resistance in the rice, not totally soft. In Italian they say "al dente," or to tooth or bite. Add the vegetables. If the rice seems almost tender, just add a small amount more stock.

Remove from heat. Add the butter and cheese to finish, mixing completely.

*Note: This dish will feed 2 as an entree or 4 as an appetizer.

www.generalstudies.newschool.edu/culinary

Miriam Brickman is a noted culinary authority, chef and educator. She began her career with her culinary foundations learned at the renown Le Cordon Bleu culinary school in Paris. With this training, Miriam found her way into the top ranks of business as executive chef in several corporate dining rooms. While her culinary prowess was appreciated, Miriam did not reach a larger audience until she arrived at The New School in New York. Working as an instructor in their respected Culinary Division, she contributed to a comprehensive culinary arts program including courses in cooking and baking, wine appreciation, and career training. No matter what the topic, Miriam consistently stressed the importance of creativity in planning, cooking and presentation.

Q: What put you on the culinary career path?
A: I came from a home with such wonderful food, I had to find a way to replicate it.

Q: Was your mother a good cook? What is your mother's best dish?
A: My grandmother and mother were fine cooks; everything was homemade. My mother's best dish was a lemon pound cake; my grandmother made incredible soups.

Q: What food could you live without and why?
A: Well, I'm forced to live without sushi because of a kidney transplant. It's hard, but I'm doing it.

BUCKWHEAT PASTA WITH POTATOES AND GREENS
PIZZOCCHERI DI TEGLIO (VALTELLINA)

BY RICCARDO BOSIO • SERVES 6

This dish brings back great memories. In the cooler months when I hiked the hills of Bergamo, Italy with my father, we would return home to this hearty dish that my mother had prepared. This is a one-pot dish, you boil the potatoes, greens and pasta all in the same pot. Mangia!

PASTA:

14 OUNCES BUCKWHEAT FLOUR (APPROXIMATELY 3⅓ CUP)

3½ OUNCES '00' WHITE FLOUR (JUST SHY OF ½ CUP)*

¼ TEASPOON FINE SEA SALT OR KOSHER SALT

5 LARGE EGGS, BEATEN
WARM WATER (OPTIONAL IF DOUGH IS TOO DRY)

BROWNED BUTTER SAUCE:

7 OUNCES BUTTER

8 FRESH WHOLE SAGE LEAVES

4 CLOVES GARLIC

14 OUNCES WAXY POTATOES, PEELED AND CUT INTO 1-INCH CUBES

14 OUNCES SAVOY CABBAGE OR SWISS CHARD, ROUGH CUT INTO 2-INCH DICE

5 OUNCES GRATED PARMIGIANO-REGGIANO CHEESE

8 OUNCES SWISS FONTINA CHEESE OR BITTO (A VALTELLINA CHEESE) CUT INTO ½-INCH CUBES

Sift the two flours and salt together in a mixer bowl. Add the eggs. Using the paddle attachment on an electric mixer, process until just blended. Turn the dough out on to a flour surface and finish kneading by hand until you have an elastic, yet firm, dough. Roll into a ball, cover with plastic wrap and let rest for 30 minutes in the refrigerator.

Divide the dough into 4 sections keeping the unrolled sections covered. Roll the dough to a ⅛-inch thickness. Cut the dough into ½ inch x 4 inch noodles. Put them on towel covered sheet pans to rest and dry for 30 minutes.

While the noodles rest, bring a large pot of well salted water to a boil. Add the peeled and diced potato and cook for 10 minutes. Add the Savoy cabbage (or Swiss chard) to the same pot and cook five minutes longer. Add the pasta to the same pot and cook al dente, approximated 7 to 10 minutes.

While the potatoes, greens and pasta are cooking you can start your sauce. In a medium frying pan, cook the butter, sage and the garlic cloves over a medium heat until the butter has turned hazelnut brown.

Once the pasta is al dente, strain the potatoes, greens and pasta well. Place in a large, warmed bowl. Add the browned butter sauce, Parmesan cheese, and Swiss Fontina (or Bitto cheese). Toss the ingredients to mix and serve.

*Note: "00" flour is a fine flour that counter balances the heaviness of the buckwheat flour.

ABOUT RICCARDO BOSIO

www.sottosopra.us
www.pazzaluna.us
www.sottocaffe.com

By 16, Riccardo Bosio had graduated from the Instituto Professionale Alberghiera di State in San Pelligrino Terme and was in the kitchen of the 5-star London Hyde Park Hotel as well as working at Michelin starred Le Gauroche under the Roux Brothers. By the time he was 17, he had been an executive chef on a private yacht off the Sardinian coast and sous chef at Cala di Volpe.

This native of Seriate, Italy in the Lombardy region near Milan did his military turn as a chef for the officers just as the Bosnian war started. By 19, Riccardo was a sous chef on The Star Princess from Portorico to the Black Sea via Barcelona, Cannes, Napoli, Venezia, Santorini, Istanbul, Odessa, and Yalta.

His career really started to flourish in his twenties when he was the sous chef at L'Enoteca on Rue Charles le V in Paris. Bosio made his way to the United States and Washington DC where he opened Sesto Sento and Duca di Milano in Chevy Chase. By 22, he was the private chef for the Italian Ambassador.

With investors after Riccardo to come to Baltimore, Sotto Sopra Restaurant was opened in 1996. By 1999 he bought out the investors to become the owner. The restaurant has received a number of awards for its contemporary Italian cuisine. Bosio is also an owner in Pazza Luna Trattoria Italiano and Sotto Caffé in Baltimore.

A vibrant personality, Riccardo will tell you to eat, drink, sleep and dream…..Italian.

Q: What is your favorite comfort food?
A: Cheese, salami, spaghetti aglio e oglio until I pass out at 4 A.M.

Q: If you were condemned to die, what would be your last meal?
A: I wouldn't eat anything, too much stress. Seriously, I would love anything my mother would love to cook for me that day, knowing it would be my last. Can you imagine the love that would transpire?

Q: If not for food, where would you be now?
A: If not for food I would rather stay in my parents thoughts and never be born.

SIMPLE ELEGANCE—FOUR-MINIT ASPARAGUS

BY SHIRLEY CORRIHER • SERVES 4

Perfectly cooked, gorgeous bright green asparagus literally in minutes.

1	POUND FRESH ASPARAGUS, RINSED IN COLD WATER
3	TABLESPOONS OLIVE OIL
½	TEASPOON SALT (SEA SALT IF POSSIBLE)
½	TEASPOON SUGAR
1	LEMON

With one hand at the root end of an asparagus stalk and the other hand three-fourths of the way up the shaft, gently bend. The asparagus will snap where the tough portion ends.

Spread asparagus out on a jelly roll pan. Drizzle with oil, then roll asparagus to coat all sides.

Slip under the broiler, about 6 inches away from the heat and broil for 4 minutes only.

Sprinkle with salt and sugar and place on serving platter or individual plates.

Using a Microplane®, grate lemon zest over the asparagus and serve immediately.

Notes: The chlorophyll in green vegetables remains bright green if vegetables are cooked less than 7 minutes.

Lemon zest is used to give a fresh lemon taste without the acidity of the lemon juice, which would turn the cooked green vegetable a yucky army drab.

Q: If you were condemned to die, what would be your last meal?
A: A lot of foie gras and truffles. Big slabs of foie gras perfectly cooked with a wonderful chutney and thin slice of brioche toast. Then a pasta with a cream sauce, once plated tossed with truffle oil and the top covered in shaved truffle to be presented in a domed covered dish so when the lid comes off you receive the most amazing aroma of truffle.

Q: What put you on the culinary career path?
A: Divorce. I had 3 small children to provide for and I would be on my feet for hours demonstrating food processors.

Q: If you could eat anywhere in the world, where would it be?
A: Where ever would give me foie gras and truffles by the sea so I could listen to the waves.

Most people recognize Shirley as the "Mad Scientist" on "Good Eats" TV show. She has appeared on "Good Eats," "Smart Solutions," "Sara Moulton Cooking Live," "Homecooking," and "Nathalie Dupree" to name a few, and once on ABC's "Jimmy Kimmel Live" with Snoop Dog as her fry chef.

Shirley Corriher was The Best Cooking Teacher of the Year in *Bon Appétit's* "Best of the Best" Annual Food and Entertaining Awards, 2001. In March 2004, Shirley received the prestigious Research Chefs' Holleman Award for outstanding achievement in technical communication. She is also in Who's Who of American Women, 2002 through present, and Who's Who.

She has long been a leading food writer and syndicated columnist. Her book *CookWise"* was the James Beard Awards winner for Best Reference and Technique Book of 1997 and has sold over 200,000 copies. Shirley was a contributing editor and wrote a regular column for *Fine Cooking* for 10 years, 1994 through 2004, and she continues to write a regular syndicated column in *The Los Angeles Times* Syndicate's Great Chefs Series (1998-present), now the *Chicago Tribune's* Media Services.

- 1997 *Cookwise* cookbook
- 2007 *Bakewise* cookbook

Q: Was your mother a good cook? What is your mother's best dish and can you duplicate it?

A: Yes my mother was an excellent cook. The dish that got passed down is the Sweet Potato Casserole which came from my paternal grandmother.

Thanksgiving Sweet Potato Casserole

Thanksgiving was always at my paternal grandmother and she made a fabulous sweet potato casserole. She would grate the raw sweet potato, mix in both dark and light brown sugar, 1 egg to bind (not too much), 3 tablespoons of cornmeal and some vanilla. Cook for about ten minutes and then stir back the drier edges to the center and the liquid center to the outer edges. Continue cooking until the casserole is set, but not dry.

(This recipe had been handed down to her grandmother and eventually to Shirley.)

HOLIDAY CRANBERRY CARROTS

RECIPE BY: JOANNA PRUESS · SERVES 8

I love carrots for their versatility and sweet flavor as well as for the color contrast they add to any plate. In this festive recipe, bags of baby carrots offer great convenience. Their orange tone is intensified by the cranberries that pop during cooking; blending with the Marsala wine to form an attractive glaze. Orange zest and cardamom add a subtle warmth and richness to the taste.

2	POUNDS BABY CARROTS
4	TABLESPOONS UNSALTED BUTTER
1½	TABLESPOONS GRATED ORANGE ZEST
¼	TEASPOON GROUND CARDAMOM
¼	CUP DRY MARSALA WINE
¾	CUP FRESH CRANBERRIES
	SALT TO TASTE

Steam the carrots until tender, about 5 to 6 minutes. Do not over-cook.

Melt the butter in a large, heavy skillet over medium-high heat. Add the carrots, orange zest, and cardamom. Cook, stirring occasionally, for 2 to 3 minutes. Add the Marsala and cranberries, turn the heat to high, and cook until the liquid has evaporated, about 3 to 5 minutes, stirring frequently. The cranberries will pop during this time. Season to taste with salt.

Note: This dish may be prepared several hours or even a day ahead of time and reheated over low heat.

ABOUT JOANNA PRUESS
(See Soups, page 124)

SPINACH WITH GARLIC, ANCHOVY, AND LEMON ZEST

BY JOYCE GOLDSTEIN • SERVES 6*

People are always raving about my spinach and asking what I do to make it so good. What I do is very little, on purpose. I melt butter in a sauté pan, turn the spinach leaves around in it until they wilt. Then I season it simply with salt and pepper. I do not add water or any liquid and I never cover the pan, which would steam the leaves, and bring up a metallic taste. By cooking the spinach uncovered, with only a bit of moisture clinging to the leaves, I end up with a tender, bright green vegetable. Spinach leaves are porous and can absorb quite a bit of butter. But you don't want to get carried away. I have given you the option for more or less butter. (Brillat Savarin writes of a legendary dish where 5 pounds of spinach absorbs 1 pound of butter, over the course of 5 days!) Try this recipe if you want people to rave about your spinach too. Don't worry about them not liking anchovy. It brings salt to the dish but is not fishy.

4 TO 6 TABLESPOONS UNSALTED BUTTER

1 TO 2 TABLESPOON FINELY MINCED ANCHOVIES

1 TABLESPOON FINELY GRATED GARLIC

2 TABLESPOONS GRATED LEMON ZEST

2 POUNDS SPINACH, LARGE STEMS REMOVED, WASHED WELL AND DRAINED

FRESHLY GROUND BLACK PEPPER

Melt the butter in a 12-inch sauté pan over medium heat. Add the anchovies, garlic, and lemon zest and cook in the butter for 2 minutes, stirring from time to time. Add the spinach. Keep stirring and turning the leaves with tongs, until they are wilted and tender. Season with pepper. The anchovies should have brought salt to the party.

   ***Note:** Serves 6 as a side dish.

ABOUT JOYCE GOLDSTEIN
(See Main Courses, page 168)

POLENTA WITH BUTTERNUT SQUASH, YAMS, OR SWEET POTATOES

BY JOYCE GOLDSTEIN • SERVES 6

This recipe combines a classic Northern Italian ravioli filling with traditional polenta. You can serve the mixture soft and creamy or pour it onto a sheet pan, refrigerate until set, and cut into strips to be sautéed or baked later. When roasting the cut squash, save clean up time by lining the sheet pan with parchment paper or a silpat. This squash or yam polenta is also a nice accompaniment for pork, ham, or poultry. Paired with cooked greens or other vegetables, it can be a satisfying meal.

2½	POUNDS BUTTERNUT SQUASH OR 2 POUNDS YAMS OR SWEET POTATOES
¼	CUP MILK
4	TABLESPOONS SOFTENED UNSALTED BUTTER
1	TEASPOON FRESHLY GRATED NUTMEG
1	PINCH GROUND CINNAMON (OPTIONAL)
	SALT AND PEPPER
2	CUPS COARSE CORNMEAL FOR POLENTA
8	CUPS WATER
1	CUP GRATED PARMESAN CHEESE
2	TO 3 TABLESPOONS CHOPPED FRESH SAGE

Preheat the oven to 400°. If using the butternut squash, cut it in half and remove the seeds before baking. Place cut side down on a sheet pan. Bake the yams, sweet potatoes or squash until soft, about 1 hour. If using yams or sweet potatoes, peel and mash. With squash, scoop out the flesh and mash or put through a ricer. Beat in milk and butter. Season with nutmeg, a pinch of cinnamon if desired, and salt and pepper. Set aside.

Combine polenta and cold water in a large saucepan over medium heat, and stirring quite often, bring to a boil. Reduce heat to low and simmer, stirring often, until thickened, about 30 minutes, or until cornmeal is no longer grainy on your tongue. Add more water if needed until polenta is cooked. Whisk in puréed squash, yams or sweet potatoes, Parmesan and chopped sage, and combine thoroughly. Season again with salt, pepper and nutmeg. Serve hot.

Or: Pour polenta onto a well-buttered baking pan (18x12x1), cover securely and refrigerate. When firm, cut into desired shapes such as triangles, rectangles, squares or strips with a knife. Use a biscuit cutter for rounds or cookie cutters for specialty shapes such as hearts (if you are feeling romantic). Dip polenta pieces in flour and sauté in butter or oil over medium heat until golden on both sides. Alternatively, place polenta pieces in buttered gratin dishes and bake in a 350 oven until hot.

Suggested wine: Rich white wine such as chardonnay, or rosé.

ABOUT JOYCE GOLDSTEIN
(See Main Courses, page 168)

GINGERY ORANGE-ROSEMARY YAMS

BY JERRY TRAUNFELD • SERVES 6

Of course this recipe shouts Thanksgiving. I first created it for my own family's holiday when I know everyone craves traditional mashed yams, but will appreciate the zing of ginger, orange, and rosemary. When it's not the third Thursday in November, serve it alongside a roast chicken, duck, or pork loin.

4	TABLESPOONS PLUS ½ TABLE-SPOON UNSALTED BUTTER
2	POUNDS YAMS OR SWEET POTATOES
1	TABLESPOON CHOPPED FRESH ROSEMARY
1	1-INCH PIECE FRESH GINGER, PEELED
1	ORANGE, PREFERABLY ORGANIC
1½	TEASPOONS KOSHER SALT
2	TABLESPOONS PLUS 2 TABLE-SPOONS CHOPPED CANDIED GINGER

Preheat the oven to 425°. Butter a shallow 1-quart baking dish with ½ tablespoon of butter or less. Roast the yams for 30 to 45 minutes, or until a paring knife can slip easily into the flesh. Remove from the oven, letting them cool until you can handle comfortably. Peel off and discard the skins. Lower the oven to 375°.

Melt the remaining 4 tablespoons butter in a small saucepan over medium heat. Stir in the rosemary. Using a zester/grater, finely grate the ginger and zest the orange. Add into the butter and cook another minute over medium-low heat. Put the yams, flavored butter, and salt in a food processor and pulse until you have a purée that still has some texture. Add 2 tablespoons of the candied ginger and pulse until incorporated. Scoop the yams into the baking dish and sprinkle with the remaining 2 tablespoons candied ginger.

This dish can be made several days ahead up to this point and refrigerated.

When ready to serve, bake the yams for about 30 minutes, or until heated through.

ABOUT JERRY TRAUNFELD

www.theherbfarm.com

As executive chef of The Herbfarm, Jerry Traunfeld combines his passion for cooking with a love of gardening and garners national attention for his innovative multi-course menus. An expert in the subject of culinary herbs, he has been featured in *The New York Times Magazine, Food and Wine, Bon Appetit, Gourmet, Fortune,* and many other publications. He has appeared on "Martha Stewart Living," Better Homes and Gardens Television, and The Food Network, and is a regular guest on Public Radio's "The Splendid Table."

After graduating from the California Culinary Academy, Jerry began his career as a pastry chef at Stars in its opening year. He moved to Seattle where he became Executive chef of the Alexis Hotel before taking his position at The Herbfarm in 1990. The Herbfarm was voted one of the nations top 10 restaurants of 2006 in Zagat, it is the only restaurant in the Northwest to be awarded 5 diamonds by AAA, and is rated one of the top 40 restaurants in the U.S for 2006 in Gayot.

Jerry is the recipient of the 2000 James Beard/American Express award for Best Chef; Northwest/Hawaii. He is the author of *The Herbfarm Cookbook,* which won The International Association of Cooking Professionals award for the Best Cookbook in the Chef/Restaurant category. His second book, *The Herbal Kitchen,* was named one of the top books of the year by *Food and Wine.*

ACHIEVEMENTS

• 2005 *The Herbal Kitchen: Cooking with Fragrance and Flavor*
• 2000 *The Herbfarm Cookbook*
• 2000 James Beard "Best Chef Northwest/Hawaii"

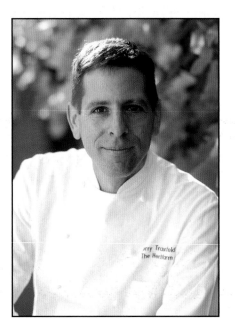

Q: What is your favorite comfort food?
A: Matzo Brie.

Q: What put you on the culinary career path?
A: I know lots of chefs have the same answer—watching Julia Child's "The French Chef " on TV when I was a kid.

Q: What is your favorite family recipe?
A: My grandmother's lekvars (Hungarian prune or apricot pastries).

BISCOTTI

BY JACQUES TORRES • FROM HIS BOOK *DESSERT CIRCUS: EXTRAORDINARY DESSERTS YOU CAN MAKE AT HOME"*
YIELD: APPROXIMATELY 5½ DOZEN BISCOTTI

The owner of Le Cirque Restaurant, Sirio Maccioni, is from a small town in Italy called Montecatini. When he invited me to visit one summer, I pictured myself lying by his pool. Instead, I met a chef from his old neighborhood and spent the day learning how to make biscotti.

Traditionally, the Italians bake biscotti two times to produce a hard cookie that they like to dip in sweet wine. I adapted the recipe so the cookie is are not quite so hard and also cut the baking time in half. I use cold butter so I can roll and bake them right away.

FOR THE BISCOTTI

¾	CUP WHOLE UNBLANCHED ALMONDS
⅓	CUP WHOLE PISTACHIOS
7	TABLESPOONS COLD UNSALTED BUTTER, CUBED
¾	CUP GRANULATED SUGAR
2	CUPS ALL-PURPOSE FLOUR
1	TABLESPOON ANISE SEEDS
1	TEASPOON BAKING POWDER
1	LEMON, ZESTED
	PINCH OF SALT
2	LARGE EGGS

FOR THE EGG WASH

1	LARGE EGG WHITE, BEATEN

Preheat the oven to 300°.

Spread the almonds and pistachios evenly on a baking sheet and place in the oven. Toast for about 30 minutes, until they are golden brown. You will be able to smell the nuts when they are ready. A good test is to break a nut in half and check to see if it is light brown on the inside. Toasting the nuts brings out their natural flavor. Remove them from the oven and allow to cool completely on the baking sheet on a wire rack.

Place the remaining ingredients in a large mixing bowl and beat with an electric mixer on medium speed until well combined, about 5 minutes. The mixture will hold together in a soft dough. Add the cooled toasted nuts and mix until they are evenly incorporated, about 1 minute. If you are using a hand-held mixer, you may want to knead in the nuts by hand to avoid burning out the motor.

Remove the dough from the mixing bowl and place on a very lightly floured work surface. If the dough is sticky and hard to work with, it is too soft. To fix this, flatten it into a disk, cover with plastic wrap, and place it in the refrigerator for a minimum of 1 hour. (When the butter in the dough gets cold, the dough will stiffen.) Remove from the refrigerator and proceed.

Preheat the oven to 350°. Divide the dough into three equal pieces. Use the palms of your hands to roll each piece on the lightly floured work surface into a rope 1 to 1½ inches in diameter.

Each rope should be even and fit on your baking sheet lengthwise. If the dough sticks to your hands or to the work surface as you are rolling it, dust it lightly with flour. Roll firmly to remove any trapped air bubbles. (At this stage, you can wrap the dough in plastic wrap and freeze for up to two weeks. Bring it back to room temperature before baking.)

Place two of the biscotti ropes on a parchment paper-covered baking sheet. You will only have room for two because they spread as they bake. With a pastry brush, lightly brush each rope with the egg white (this will add shine to the baked biscotti). Bake until golden brown, about 30 minutes. Remove from the oven and let cool slightly on the baking sheet.

Use a serrated knife to slice the biscotti on a diagonal into ½-inch-thick cookies. If you do this while the biscotti are still warm, they will not crumble. The biscotti will harden as they cool. If they are still soft when you slice them, place the slices on a baking sheet and bake at 300° for another 10 to 15 minutes. Repeat the baking and cooling procedure with the remaining biscotti rope.

Store in an airtight container at room temperature for two to three weeks.

Serving suggestion: These fragrant, flavorful cookies are great by themselves or dunked in coffee. Since I'm from Provence, I prefer to dip mine in pastis.

Optional: Dip the biscotti halfway on a diagonal into tempered bittersweet chocolate. Wipe the excess chocolate from the tip and place the biscotti on a sheet of parchment paper to allow the chocolate to set.

ABOUT JACQUES TORRES

www.mrchocolate.com

Jacques Torres grew up in Bandol, France, a small town in the southern region of Provence. In 1980, he landed a job with Michelin two-star chef Jacques Maximin at the Hotel Negresco and started a relationship that would last 8 years and take him around the globe. In 1986, Jacques was awarded with the prestigious M.O.F. medal, the youngest chef to earn the distinction.

In 1988, he ventured to the America, becoming the Corporate Pastry Chef for Ritz Carlton. In 1989, the legendary Sirio Maccioni invited Jacques to work at New York's Le Cirque. For 11 years, Jacques served presidents, kings, and celebrities.

In 2000, Jacques fulfilled a life-long dream and opened his first chocolate factory, Jacques Torres Chocolate in Brooklyn, specializing in fresh, hand-crafted chocolates free of preservatives and artificial flavors. His creations utilize state-of-the-art technology and production techniques, all of which is visible through the plate glass windows in the factory.

In 2004, he opened a second chocolate factory in downtown New York City. Here, Jacques unravels the mystery of chocolate, showcasing the process of turning cocoa beans and into chocolate bars.

He serves as Dean of Pastry Studies at New York's French Culinary Institute. He is also author of two cookbooks and host of his own television shows. Jacques always finds time for philanthropic endeavors and press appearances. He is currently busy on a new chocolate book, his next TV series, a third retail location and as always, new creations in chocolate.

ACHIEVEMENTS

- 1998 *Dessert Circus at Home* cookbook (Harper Collins)
- 1997 *Dessert Circus* cookbook (Harper Collins)

Q: If you could meet Auguste Escoffier, what would you ask him?
A: What came first, the chicken or the egg?

Q: What put you on the culinary career path?
A: My true love of food put me to a career in pastry.

Q: If not for food, where would you be now?
A: I would be sailing around the world on a boat.

Q: If you could eat anywhere in the world, where would it be?
A: El Bulli in Spain.

BISCOTTI

JACQUES TORRES CHOCOLATE

APPLE CROSTATA WITH WALNUTS AND TIPSY CREAM

BY LESLIE MEYER • SERVES 6

CRUST

1¼	CUP FLOUR
1	TABLESPOON SUGAR
½	TEASPOON SALT
1	TEASPOON LEMON ZEST
4	OUNCES COLD UNSALTED BUTTER, CUT INTO 8 PIECES
4	TO 6 TABLESPOONS ICE WATER

FILLING

4	GOLDEN DELICIOUS APPLES OR COOKING APPLE OF YOUR CHOICE, PEELED, CORED AND SLICED INTO ½-INCH SLICES
⅓	CUP PLUS 1 TABLESPOON SUGAR
½	TEASPOON CINNAMON
⅛	TEASPOON FRESHLY GRATED NUTMEG
2	TABLESPOONS FLOUR
¼	CUP WALNUTS, COARSELY CHOPPED
1	EGG YOLK, BEATEN
1	TABLESPOON HEAVY CREAM

TIPSY CREAM

1	CUP HEAVY WHIPPING CREAM
2	TO 3 TABLESPOONS CONFECTIONERS SUGAR
	SPLASH CAVADOS (OR OTHER APPLE FLAVORED LIQUEUR)

For the crust: Combine the flour, 1 tablespoon of sugar, salt and lemon zest in a food processor and pulse to blend. Add the butter and pulse until the mixture forms coarse crumbs. Empty the crumbs into a medium sized bowl. Sprinkle about 4 tablespoons of ice water over top.

With a rubber spatula, mix the crumbs until the mixture forms a dough, adding more water as needed. With your hands, shape the dough into a 1-inch-thick disk. Wrap the disk tightly in plastic wrap and refrigerate for at least 30 minutes.

Preheat an oven to 425° F

For the filling: Combine the apples, ⅓ cup of sugar, cinnamon, nutmeg, flour, and walnuts in a bowl and toss well.

For assembly: Place the dough round on floured surface and roll into a 12- to 13-inch round (about a ¼-inch thickness), flouring the round and the surface lightly as needed to keep the dough from sticking. Carefully move the dough to a cookie sheet. Fill the center of the dough round with the apple mixture in an even layer, leaving a border of about 1½ inches. Fold the border up and over the apples to make a rim. Mix the egg yolk and heavy cream together to make an egg wash. Brush the rim of the crostata with egg wash and then sprinkle with 1 tablespoon of sugar.

For the tipsy cream: Whip the heavy cream with until stiff. Whisk in 2 to 3 tablespoons of confectioner's sugar and splash of the Calvados or other apple-flavored liqueur.

Bake the crostata until the crust is nicely browned and the apples are bubbling, about 40 minutes. Let stand for about 15 minutes before serving. Serve warm with a dollop of the Tipsy Cream.

Note: The Crostata can be made hours ahead and reheated before serving. To reheat, place in a 375° oven for 10 to 15 minutes or until warmed through.

ABOUT LESLIE MEYER
www.moonlightcuisine.com
(See Main Courses, page 189)

LEMON SCENTED CHOCOLATE TART

BY NICK MALGIERI • SERVES 8

Cocoa Pastry Dough

1	CUP ALL-PURPOSE FLOUR (SPOON FLOUR INTO DRY-MEASURE CUP AND LEVEL OFF)
3	TABLESPOONS ALKALIZED (DUTCH PROCESS) COCOA, SIFTED AFTER MEASURING
¼	CUP SUGAR
¼	TEASPOON SALT
½	TEASPOON BAKING POWDER
5	TABLESPOONS UNSALTED BUTTER, COLD, CUT INTO 10 PIECES
1	LARGE EGG

Lemony Chocolate Filling

1	CUP HEAVY WHIPPING CREAM
⅓	CUP SUGAR
6	TABLESPOONS UNSALTED BUTTER (¾ STICK) CUT INTO 12 PIECES
4	OUNCES BITTERSWEET (NOT UNSWEETENED) CHOCOLATE, CUT INTO ¼-INCH PIECES
3	OUNCES MILK CHOCOLATE, CUT INTO ¼-INCH PIECES
3	LARGE EGGS
1	TABLESPOON FINELY GRATED LEMON ZEST
⅛	TEASPOON GROUND CINNAMON
1	10-INCH FLUTED TART PAN WITH REMOVABLE BOTTOM

For the dough: Combine the flour, cocoa, sugar, salt, and baking powder in the bowl of a food processor fitted with the metal blade. Pulse 5 or 6 times to mix. Add the butter and pulse repeatedly until the butter is finely mixed in. Add the egg and continue pulsing until the dough forms a ball.

Invert the dough to a floured work surface and carefully remove the blade. Form the dough into a disk and flour it lightly. Roll the dough to a 12-inch disk, moving it frequently and adding more flour under and on the dough as necessary.

Fold the dough in half and transfer it to the pan, supporting it underneath with the palms of both hands, lining up the fold with the diameter of the pan. Unfold the dough and press it well into the bottom and sides of the pan. Use a bench scraper or the back of a paring knife to sever any excess dough at the rim of the pan. Chill the crust while preparing the filling.

Set a rack in the lowest level of the oven and preheat to 350°.

For the filling: Combine the cream and sugar in a medium saucepan and whisk to mix. Place over low heat and bring to a simmer. Add the butter, and continue to cook until it melts completely. Remove the pan from the heat and add both chocolates. Shake the pan and let it stand for 3 or 4 minutes.

Combine the eggs, lemon zest, and cinnamon in a mixing bowl and whisk to mix. Whisk the chocolate and cream mixture smooth, then whisk it into the egg mixture in a stream, mixing only until it is just combined. Pour the filling into the crust smooth the top. Bake the tart until the crust is baked through and the filling is set, about 30 to 35 minutes. Cool the tart on a rack.

Unmold the tart to a platter and cover it loosely. Keep the tart at room temperature until you intend to serve it. For advance preparation, wrap and refrigerate the tart and bring it to room temperature for several hours before serving.

ABOUT NICK MALGIERI
www.nickmalgieri.com
(See Brunch, page 86)

CARAMEL CUSTARD WITH GINGER AND HAZELNUT

BY FRANCOIS DIONOT · SERVES 6

FOR CARAMEL

1   CUP SUGAR
¼   CUP WATER

FOR CUSTARD

1   INCH FRESH GINGER, PEELED
1   CUP WHOLE PEELED HAZELNUTS
2   CUPS HALF AND HALF
3   EGGS
2   EGG YOLKS
4   OUNCES SUGAR (½ CUP)
1   TEASPOON VANILLA EXTRACT

In a pan smaller than the heat source, heat 1 cup of sugar and water (well mixed) and bring to a boil. Cook (over med heat) until the liquid achieves a caramel or amber color. Pour into 5 ounce glass custard cups to cover the bottom.

Grate the ginger, saving all of the juices.

Grind the hazelnuts fine in a food processor.

Bring the half and half to a boil.

Mix the eggs, egg yolks, and 4 ounces (½ cup) of sugar very well. Pour the hot half and half into the egg mixture whisking constantly. Add the vanilla, ginger and hazelnuts.

Fill each custard cup with the custard. Set the custard cups in a shallow, oven-proof dish lined with a double layer of paper towels. Pour hot water into the oven-proof dish so that it comes up the sides of the custard cups.

Bake the custards in this bain marie (water bath) at 325° for 40 minutes or until set. (Note: Ovens vary so keep an eye that these don't over cook.)

When set, remove the custard dishes from oven to cool, then refrigerate. Custard is best unmolded 2 days later as all of the caramel will have melted again.

To unmold, run a table knife around the edge and invert on to a serving plate. You may need to give it a little shake.

Francois Dionot is the Founder, Owner and Director of L'Academie de Cuisine. Since the school's inception in 1976, he has been teaching the theoretical components of cooking and working in the food service industry, conducting recreational French cooking courses and preparing elaborate "Great Dinners."

Francois grew up in Reims, France, studying and serving culinary apprenticeships in both France and Switzerland. He earned a diploma in hotel and restaurant management and the culinary arts at the prestigious L'Ecole Hotelière de la Sociéte Suisse des Hoteliers in Lausanne, Switzerland. He was lured to Washington DC by Hotel Sonesta to manage their food and beverage operations. After working in several other positions, and recognizing a need for a formal European-style culinary institution, he opened L'Academie de Cuisine, recently voted one of America's ten best culinary schools.

In addition to operating L'Academie de Cuisine, Francois conducts master classes for organizations including the Food Editors Association and the Home Economists Association. He was a consulting chef for Time-Life Books' The Good Cook series, and frequently appears on television. He most recently taught on the QEII with Julia Child and Andre Soltner as part of Cunard's Chef Palette Educational Program.

Francois is a founding member and past president of the IACP. In 1997, L'Academie de Cuisine received the IACP's Award of Excellence in the cooking school category. Francois is also a member of The James Beard Foundation and a James Beard awards judge since 1995. He is a Commandeur, Conseiller Culinaire provincial of the international Confréries de la Châine des Rotisseurs, and a member of the American Institute of Wine and Food.

Q: What is your favorite comfort food?
A: Coq au vin.

Q: If not for food, where would you be now?
A: Race car driver.

Q: Was your mother a good cook? What is your mother's best dish and can you duplicate it?
A: Yes, she was a good cook. Tarte aux pommes was her best dish and yes, I can duplicate it.

ABOUT NANCY BAGGETT

www.kitchenlane.com

Nancy Baggett is an award-winning cookbook author, food journalist and culinary researcher with sixteen cookbooks and hundreds of food articles to her credit. Nancy's latest cookbooks include her 2001 bestselling *The All-American Cookie Book*, a James Beard and IACP best baking book nominee, and *The All-American Dessert Book*, which made *The New York Times'* "Notable Cookbooks of 2005" list and was called "elegant and inspiring" by *Publishers Weekly*.

An authority on American culinary history and best known for her desserts and sweets recipes, she has contributed to *Bon Appetit, Gourmet, Food & Wine, Eating Well, Woman's Day, Fine Cooking, The Washington Post,* and many other publications. She has also been a guest chef and culinary expert on "Today," "Good Morning America," the "Early Show," NPR's "All Things Considered," the History Channel's "What America Eats," as well as on television satellite tours and scores of other radio and television shows.

Nancy Baggett trained as a pastry chef with former White House Executive Pastry Chef Roland Mesnier. She holds a BA in English and MS in Communications. She is a member of the Washington, DC chapter of Les Dames d'Escoffier; The International Association of Culinary Professionals; and the Home Baking Association.

ACHIEVEMENTS

Three of Nancy Baggett's cookbooks have received "best book" nominations from the International Association of Culinary Professionals. Most recently, *The All-American Cookie Book* was honored with best book nominations from both the IACP and the James Beard Foundation. Nancy's 1991 work, *The International Chocolate Cookbook* was chosen the IACP's Best Book in the Baking and Desserts category.

OLIVE OIL CAKE

BY JAMIE GWEN • SERVES 12

3   LARGE EGGS, BEATEN
2   CUPS GRANULATED SUGAR
12   OUNCES EXTRA-VIRGIN OLIVE
         OIL*
10   OUNCES WHOLE MILK
¼   CUP ORANGE LIQUEUR
¼   CUP FRESH ORANGE JUICE
3   TEASPOONS FRESHLY ZESTED
         MEYER OR REGULAR LEMON
2   CUPS ALL-PURPOSE FLOUR
½   TEASPOON BAKING SODA
½   TEASPOON BAKING POWDER
¼   TEASPOON FRESHLY GRATED
         NUTMEG
1   TEASPOON KOSHER SALT
4   OUNCES BLANCHED ALMONDS,
         FINELY CHOPPED

GARNISH: POWDERED SUGAR

7-MINUTE LEMON, ORANGE, OR
PASSIONFRUIT CURD (SEE PAGE
266)

Preheat the oven to 350°. Butter a 10-inch cake pan.

In a large bowl, whisk together the eggs, sugar, olive oil, milk, liqueur, orange juice and lemon zest. In another bowl, sift together the flour, baking soda, baking powder, nutmeg and salt. Mix the dry mixture into the wet mixture. Whisk until well blended. Fold in the almonds.

Pour the mixture into the buttered cake pan. Bake for 1 hour or until a cake tester inserted in the center of the cake comes out clean.

Place on a rack to cool completely then remove the cake from the pan by inverting onto a serving platter. Dust the top of the cake with powdered sugar and serve with the 7-Minute Curd (see page 266).

*Note: Using extra virgin olive oil in this cake results in a fruity and rich flavor.

CITRUS VINAIGRETTE

BY SUSANNA FOO • FROM HER BOOK *SUSANNA FOO FRESH INSPIRATION*
YIELDS: 1¼ CUPS

This recipe, used with my Belgian Endive Salad (see Salads, page 127), is my favorite salad dressing. The base is fresh orange and lime juice. Cooking the vinaigrette to reduce not only concentrates the flavor but also means the dressing can be stored for much longer in the refrigerator. Adding a little dissolved cornstarch helps prevent the separation of oil and vinegar that often occurs in homemade salad dressings.

	GRATED ZEST OF ½ ORANGE
	GRATED ZEST OF ½ LIME
2	CUPS FRESH ORANGE JUICE
¼	CUP FRESH LIME JUICE
¼	TEASPOON CORNSTARCH MIXED WITH 1 TEASPOON WATER
2	TABLESPOONS MINCED SHALLOTS
1	TABLESPOON FINELY CHOPPED ROSEMARY
½	CUP EXTRA VIRGIN OLIVE OIL
1	TABLESPOON KOSHER SALT
	FRESH GROUND WHITE PEPPER

Combine the zests, orange juice, lime juice and cornstarch mixture in a medium saucepan and bring to a boil, then lower the heat to a simmer and cook uncovered until reduced to 1 cup, about 20 minutes). Remove from heat and let cool. Pour the cooled liquid into a blender and add the shallots and rosemary. While the motor is running, slowly drizzle in the olive oil until the vinaigrette is emulsified. Season with salt and white pepper to taste.

Store in a glass jar with a tight-fitting lid. The dressing can be refrigerated for about 2 weeks.

Note: This dressing goes well with other bitter-greens or fruit salads.

ABOUT SUSANNA FOO
www.susannafoo.com
(See Salads, page 128)

CRANBERRY-TERIYAKI GLAZE

BY MING TSAI • FROM HIS BOOK *MING'S MASTER RECIPES*
YIELDS 3 CUPS

This recipe is used in Cranberry-Teriyaki Lamb (see Main Courses, page 159).

1	LARGE RED ONION, SLICED
1	TABLESPOON MINCED GINGER
1	CUP DRIED CRANBERRIES
	ZEST AND JUICE OF 1 ORANGE
1	CUP NATURALLY BREWED SOY SAUCE
2	CUPS CRANBERRY JUICE
½	CUP SUGAR
¼	CUP GRAPESEED OR CANOLA OIL FOR COOKING
	KOSHER SALT AND FRESHLY GROUND BLACK PEPPER

In a sauce pan coated lightly with oil on high heat, sauté the onions, ginger and dried cranberries until soft, about 5 minutes.

Add the orange zest and juice, naturally brewed soy sauce, cranberry juice, and sugar and bring to a simmer. Reduce by 50 percent over low heat, about 10 to 15 minutes. Check for flavor.

Immediately transfer to a blender and blend until almost smooth (a few remaining small bits is preferable), drizzling in the oil. Take care to not blend super smooth.

Check for flavor and adjust seasonings. Let come to room temperature. Transfer to a glass jar, seal and store in fridge.

ABOUT MING TSAI
www.ming.com
(See Main Courses, page 160)

KITCHEN SHOTS

(THE TESTERS)